DEATH
and the
LIFE
HEREAFTER

"Our eyes shall see the beauty and the glory of the King."

DEATH
and the
LIFE HEREAFTER

Herbert Lockyer

BAKER BOOK HOUSE
Grand Rapids, Michigan

Copyright 1967 by Herbert Lockyer
Reprinted 1975 by Baker Book House
with permission of the copyright owner

ISBN: 0-8010-5551-2

First printing, April 1975
Second printing, February 1977

Formerly published under the title
The Gospel of the Life Beyond

Printed in the United States of America

CONTENTS

6 *Contents*

CHAPTER ONE

The Fascination of the Great Beyond

IT is to our great loss that we fail to live under the influence of eternal verities. Like the man with the muck-rake with his eyes searching the dirt of earth for worthless articles, yet failing to see the Crown of gold above his head, we, too, are earth-bound. Our minds are set on things below and not on the more glorious and enduring treasures above. Living as if we are to be on this planet for ever, we forget that our days vanish as a shadow, and that beyond the grave there is ETERNITY. Ours is not the song Bishop Heber left us to sing:

"Our heart is in Heaven, our home is not here."

True, human life is most exhilarating and there is so much exciting discovery and romantic adventure here and now, so why be concerned about a distant hereafter? When a dear one crosses the barrier and heart and home are left vacant then we pause to think where we are going rather than where we are, and interest is awakened in what has happened to the one "we loved and lost awhile". Many questions clamour for an answer. Where has our beloved one gone? What is he or she doing? Can the precious dead see and hear us? Are consciousness and memory retained? The question George MacDonald asked is one we all ask when we face the overwhelming experience of loss and sorrow:

Traveller, what lies over the hill?
    Traveller, tell to me;
I am only a child—from the window-sill,
    Over I cannot see.

7

Too often, however, the loneliness of parting passes, and Time the Healer covers the wound, and gradually we think less of the distant scene. Back to the present we come, with questions of a future life no longer uppermost and pressing for answers. But for the true Christian, there should be the constant remembrance that he is only a stranger and a pilgrim in this world, and that Heaven is his home. The joy, the wonder, the exuberance of a never-ending life in the Saviour's presence should always possess his mind for in such a heavenly hope there is a blessed serenity. If Heaven is ever in his heart, then at death he will go bounding Home as a schoolboy does when classes and lessons are over, and he hastens home to the dear ones awaiting his coming.

What is wrong with those of us who believe that our citizenship is already in Heaven? Where is the thrill, the wonder, the eager anticipation John expressed, when, as an old man of some ninety years of age, he was yet like an eager youth awaiting a glorious adventure, when he exclaimed:

"It doth not yet appear what we shall be!" 1 John 3: 2. A life with such a vision is emancipated from the dreary, monotonous feeling gripping many today. Outlook gives zest to life and enables us to cram earth with Heaven. Living with our eyes on the far horizon does not make us indifferent to our present obligations. We do not become so heavenly-minded as to be of no earthly use. The joy set before us enables us to face life's trials with a calm resignation and inspires us to pack the very best into the little while between. As each day's work ends and we nightly pitch our tent, our hearts are elate with the glorious thought that it is another day's march nearer Home: and that the days are not accumulating before us as they are behind us. Each one is less. "A sunset nearer every night; a sunset nearer glory bright."

Our prayer should be for a more constant contemplation of the blest estate awaiting us, and of the country in which sickness, pain, sorrow, farewells and death are unknown. How enthused we ought to be over such a land in which no eyes are ever wet with tears, and brows never have a shade or wrinkle, and limbs never tire in the service of the King! There, fear and dread are unknown, and the inhabitants "count not time by years, for there is no night there". Danson Smith carries such a sentiment in the verse:

> There is no night of things unknown, uncertain;
>> Things which now try the heart to make it strong.
> There is no night—there is no veiling curtain—
>> Just light, and bliss, and joy, and endless song.

Awaiting such a glorious consummation does not mean that we will wait indolently. No, the scenes of a sweeter day will serve to wean our hearts from so much that is empty in the present changing world-order, and fix them upon the heavenly and eternal. "If this is done we shall live well here by living much there; we shall have a truer perspective, and worthier sense of values. We shall not mistake imitation gems for priceless jewels; nor shall we throw away eternal gains for momentary gains. To live well in this world we must be other-worldly", as Dr. Graham Scroggie reminds us. "Time is our opportunity to prepare for Eternity, and this world is the sphere in which to qualify for the next." In Faber's familiar hymn in which Heaven is spiritualized as *Paradise*, the hymnist gives expression to the yearning in every redeemed heart for our Home "above the bright blue sky":

> O Paradise, O Paradise,
>> I greatly long to see
> The special place my dearest Lord
>> Is destining for me:
> Where loyal hearts and true
>> Stand ever in the light,
> All rapture thro' and thro'
>> In God's most holy sight.

Already, through grace, in the heavenlies where our life is hid with Christ in God, may we be found living out our days below with the upward gaze. Then, whether we go Home by the way of a grave or by way of the air, when Jesus comes, it will make no difference for, to adapt the well-known lines:

> O think!
> To step on shore,
>   And that shore Heaven!
> To take hold of a Hand,
>   And that Christ's Hand!
> To breathe a new air,
>   And feel it celestial air!
> To feel invigorated,
>   And know it immortality!
> O think!
> To pass from the storms and the tempest
>   To one unbroken calm!
> To wake up
>   And find it Glory!

The eighteenth-century poet, William Allingham, has the couplet in his *Poems*:

> His blissful soul was in Heaven, though a
>   breathing man was he;
> He was out of time's dominion, so far as the
>   living may be.

May we be found while still in "time's dominion", living and labouring in the light of that summer land up yonder, ever remembering that, "When a man from the contemplation of heavenly things brings himself to consider things human, he will certainly speak and feel everything in a higher and nobler manner!"

CHAPTER TWO

The Instinct of Savage and Saint

BELIEF in a life beyond the grave is all but universal. It is well-nigh impossible to find a tribe of the lowest nature that does not have faith in some form of existence after death—that Mother Earth is not man's final resting place. When the Eternal God created Adam and Eve, He wove into their nature the hope of immortality which the succeeding centuries of sin and darkness were not able to completely erase from man's inner being. Such a homing instinct was imparted by God Who "planted Eternity in men's hearts and minds", Eccles. 3: 11, see R.V.M. and *Amplified Bible*. Solomon might not have known whether the spirit of man goes upward, and the spirit of a beast downward (Eccles. 3: 21), but he certainly knew that God had put into man's heart not only the consciousness of his limitations, but something that takes him beyond them and speaks of eternal expansion.

Nature never betrays the instinct of the future within birds and beasts. The unborn chick longs to break its shell-environment, thus finding itself in another, larger world. So man has a deep-rooted instinct that all his God-given powers must find the fullest expression and perfection elsewhere. The instinct of the swallow is also remarkable. As autumn dawns, they gather together from every quarter, and the night comes when the air is thick with them, chirping, as if in conference as to the long flight ahead. The next morning, not one swallow can be found, for during the night the winged host crossed the sea to spend the winter in Africa, or the south of Europe, or some other warmer clime. Probably one half of those swallows had never flown that way before, seeing they were hatched out in early summer in the land they came to leave, but a mysterious inner voice called them away from winter with its cold and frost and snow to a sunnier land.

Surely a saint is not less endowed than a swallow? Are our instincts after a fuller life and a fairer clime to be mocked? No! Then thousand times, No! The homing instinct God wrought into man's nature will not be betrayed or mocked. "He is not ashamed to be called their God. For He hath prepared for them a city" (Heb. 11: 14–16). Instinct cheers the empty heart of the bereaved mother with the hope that the babe she laid away with tears is blossoming in another world, and that as love never dies, she will once again clasp her child to her breast. Instinct assures the desolate widow that her beloved husband who, from their union, had been her shield, and into whose heart she poured her affection, awaits her arrival in the palace of the King. Instinct consoles the lonely husband with the thought that the partner for so long, whose love and smile made home for him, and whose passing robbed life of its chief attraction, has only crossed the bar a little beforehand. Although half of his heart is in Heaven, he is comforted by the assurance of a blissful reunion. Sir W. Robertson Nicoll in his volume, *The Key of The Grave*, tells the following story of a factory girl he heard of:

"I think if this should be the end of all; and if all I have been poor for is just to work my heart and life away in this dull place, with these mill-stones in my ears forever, until I could scream out for them to stop and let me have a little quiet; with my mother gone, and I never able to tell her again how I loved her, and of all my troubles—I think if this life is the end and there is no God to wipe away all tears from all eyes, *I would go mad*."

There are multitudes more who, because of their cramped circumstances here below feel the same way. Yet they endure because they see Him Who is invisible, and whose word about a world in which there is no want, no stress or strain, consoles their hearts. Even Logic, akin to Reason, suggests one of the strongest arguments, apart from the Bible, for immortality. Who can watch by a deathbed and believe in extinction, especially when the dying one is enabled to cross the chilly waters of death sustained by vision and voices from the other side? Transition to another world is overwhelmingly borne in upon one's mind as we witness the old house being vacated and the tenant leaving for another country. Before we come to the scriptural evidence regarding the indestructibility of personality, let us take a look at the witness of the races to the continuity of existence after death.

Professor James Orr in his great work, *The Christian View of God*, reminds us "that nearly every tribe and people on the face of the earth, savage and civilized, has held in some form this belief in a future state of existence". Writing on their catholic belief, M. Renouff expresses a similar observation: "A belief in the persistence of life after death and the observance of religious practices founded upon the belief, may be discovered in every part of the world, in every age, and among men representing every degree and variety of culture." Pagan ideas may appear to be crude, but the crudity does not invalidate the value of the ideas. While we cannot squeeze perfect conceptions of Eternity into the band-box of one generation or many, and no two nations may agree as to the exact nature of the after-life, nevertheless the light is there, although it may not be as full as we have it. Does this not prove that "Christ was not the *first* to stamp the truth of immortality on the minds of men under the forms of Heaven and Hell? Christ nowhere asserts, neither is it asserted for Him by those He commissioned to speak in His name, that the truth which He inculcated was something wholly novel and without antecedents." What is claimed for Him Who came as "The Truth" was that He "brought life and immortality to *light* through the Gospel" (2 Tim. 1: 10)—which He did by giving lucidity to what was obscure; completeness to what was fragmentary; certainty to what was probable; perfection to the partial.

In connection with the witness of Heathendom to man's survival beyond the tomb we have what Professor Salmond calls "the ethnic preparation" for the incontrovertible proof of immortality coming down to us on monuments, and in rites and beliefs, all of which declare that:

> In even savage bosoms
> There are longings, yearnings, strivings
> For the good they comprehend not;
> That the feeble hands and helpless,
> Groping blindly in the darkness,
> Touch God's right hand in that darkness,
> And are lifted up and strengthened.

Thinking of the testimony of monuments, we have the Pyramids of Egypt which are among the marvels of the world. For generations, men have been astounded at the human skill and labour involved in the erection of these remarkable structures. But what was the reason for these strange and enduring, mighty mounds of stone? Was it not the declaration of the Egyptian belief in the survival of the soul? Egyptians believed that the souls of the departed were in some way still connected with the bodies they had left, and that, periodically, they would return to them. Other nations erected their "house tombs", built in the form of chambers because it was believed that the dead still lived and revisited their tombs, which were thus made pleasant for their return.

Further, heathen rites and incantations performed at burial places witness to the same belief in another life and world. Mary Slessor found in West Africa that when a chief died, his wives and slaves were put to death and buried with him in the belief that the tribal chief was yet alive and needed his wives and slaves where he had gone.

The Indian mother expresses the same faith when, after the death of her child, she repairs each morning to the little grave and places a saucer of milk thereon for the child's nourishment wherever he is. Likewise, the Indian warrior was buried with his bow and arrow for the continuation of his hunting where he had gone. The oldest piece of literature in the world is the Egyptian *Book of The Dead*, which is an extraordinary collection of prayers and formulae for the guidance and protection of the deceased in the after-world.

The Egyptians, who believed intensely in the continuance of life, had the repute, Professor Salmond tells us, of being the first people to teach the immortality of the soul. The oldest inscription given to a coffin was "the chest of the living", for the Egyptians believed that the reanimation of the body was essential to perfected existence, hence, the practice of embalming and the placing of statuettes of the deceased in the tomb. Seeds of grain were also enclosed with the body as if, with prophetic ear, they had heard the words, "That which thou sowest is not quickened, except it die" (1 Cor. 15: 36–38). The hands of dead children would be filled with trinkets and toys and inscribed upon their Cryssus bands there was the hope of eternity. It was also taught that the dead descended to an underworld where they were judged by Osiris and his forty-two assessors. As souls were weighed in the scales of justice—the good, going to the god of light—the bad, to the god of darkness. None were exterminated, but all passed onward to a future life. The Egyptians also taught the migration of souls—the soul of a person who had died passing into one animal, then into another, until it had circled through all forms of the animal creation and finally emerged in human form again. The whole period of this transmigration lasted about three thousand years.

The Babylonians were likewise religious in their way and had their conception of existence beyond the grave. That they believed in the resurrection of the dead can be gathered from one of their hymns to their deity, *Mero-dach*:

> Merciful one among the gods,
> Merciful one, who restores the dead to life.

The dead had to appear naked before the god of the underworld where he, as judge, determined their lot, sending the condemned to a place of imprisonment and pain. For heroes, there was transportation to a happy resting-place. The most a Babylonian could hope for was entrance into "the land of the silver sky", and to him the world of the dead was a world of ghosts called by a variety of names such as, The lower earth, The great city, The house of darkness, The land of no return. Both the Babylonians and the Assyrians conceived of the abode of the dead as a great city, having seven encircling walls, and a river flowing around or through it. Babylonians buried their dead with jars containing food and drink, dates and other fruits, wine and liquors. Men were buried with their token of office at their hand, and women had their combs and cosmetics.

The Persians had modes of thought and belief which Professor Salmond affirms gave form and colour to early Bible expressions. Persian faith of immortality had a singularly clear and decisive doctrine of future retribution, and a profound conception of good and of guilt. There was also a rigid and peculiar idea on the subject of the disposal of their dead, such as the exposure of the naked body, "clothed only with the Light of Heaven". Bodies were exposed to become the food of bird or beast, but the soul crossed over the Bridge of Chinvat, or The Bridge of the Gatherer or Accountant. Then, for three days, good spirit and evil, Paradise and Hell struggled for the possession of the soul. After the final reckoning, the good life of a man of truth appeared in the form of a fair maiden of glorious race while for the man of falsehood there was a corresponding apparition of the evil things of his dissolute, earthly life. If good, the man passed into the abode of song; if evil, he fell into the abyss tenanted by the spirits of evil, "down into darkness of the earth-spirit, down into the world of woe, the dismal realm, down into the House of Hell".

The Grecians, as no other peoples have, left their mark upon a wide world of thought. To the quick, sensitive Greek, life was joy, with the world its genuine scene and proper minister. To be alive on earth was to *live*, but death was the sorest of ills because it took man away from earth and life. Yet the Grecian believed that death was not the end of man. Something survived. The mass of men, it was taught, pass into Hades, good and evil, slave and prince alike. Rewards and punishments were distributed by the gods, corresponding to the good or evil fortune on this side of death. There was the Island of the Blest where warriors rested from battle. The Grecian poet, *Findas*, taught that souls went down to Hades, atoned for past offences, and returned to earth to become great or wise men, or heroes. *Plato*, the Greek prophet of the Ideal and the Eternal, carried to a loftier height the belief of the persistence of the soul in right-doing, seeing that there was a judgment after death for all souls according to their deeds on earth; a Heaven for the pure and a Hell for the impure. *Socrates*, the famous Athenian preacher and philosopher, believed in immortality. We are all familiar with the episode when the sun touched the horizon, and Socrates, condemned to die, draining the poisoned cup of hemlock, exclaimed: "If the common expression be true that death conveys us to the place of departed men, with delight I drink this hemlock, for it sends my spirit to commune with Ajax and Palamedes." As his disciples asked their master where he wished to be buried, he replied in words that became immortal: "Bury *me*, if you can catch *me*."

Natives of Central Africa had their different, tribal interpretations of immortality. Alexander Mackay, pioneer missionary of the Church Missionary Society to Uganda, wrote of the custom of laying the dead in a uniform direction, east and west, in their graves, the belief being that at death the soul went to its new abode in the west, the way of the setting sun. Perhaps it was this custom that gave rise to the phrase so often used of those who died in the last World War—*Gone West!* Mackay also reminds us how the African widows took up their residence near the house-tomb in order to be near "all their days to watch the departed spirit". It was likewise believed that these bereaved women not only held converse with the departed husband, but also possessed his spirit.

American Indians, although barbarians, expressed their belief in an after-life. In their funeral customs they were akin to the Egyptians in that they buried their dead with bow and arrow in hope of a happy hunting ground hereafter.

The Hindu Uttarakura proclaim the land of the blessed and use remarkable imagery to describe the felicity of those who pass over. There are lakes, golden beds of red lotus, pearls and jewels on the banks of rivers instead of sand, song and music and laughter with pleasant qualities growing brighter every day.

The Japanese have their "plain of high Heaven" where all the great men, heroes, midados, and famous, dwell with the gods in a Heaven minutely described as being more beautiful and extensive than anything found on earth. In the Western Paradise of Japanese Buddhists, "the Happy or Blissful Land is a state where there is neither mental nor bodily pain, for pleasure is universal; the name of Hell is unknown, and the length of life is immeasurable". The Buddhist likewise employs rich language and metaphor to describe the bliss of this glorious, fertile and beautiful Paradise which he enters at death.

The Iranians believe in a Hell for the sinner, and a Heaven for the virtuous, with their Heaven being "a house of song", "the kingdom of blessing", "the best existence", and "the everlasting lights", as well as the sphere of ineffable bliss.

The Mohammedans have a belief in the after-life which greatly appeals to the Arab of the desert, namely that of luxury, pleasure and rest. The Koran description of the blissful abode for the Mohammedan tells us

"Paradise is better than anything in the world."

One could continue with further evidence from other peoples of all ages who, widely separated geographically, culturally, intellectually, religiously and socially, yet believed in a life beyond the present one, and in a Heaven for the worthy. In his work of *Primitive Culture*, Dr. Taylor says that: "Looking at the religion of the lower races as a whole we shall at least not be ill-advised in taking as one of its general and principal elements the doctrine of the soul's future life." With endless diversity of detail this idea was universal among pagans from the primitive savage to the cultured Greek and Roman.

With our Christian outlook on the life to come we may smile at the way the heathen has expressed immortality, but surely such a hope is not a mirage? Such a God-planted intuition is not in man to mock him. Speaking broadly, mankind from the beginning has had a conviction—mysterious, startling, usually more vivid as moral forces became more active in the life—that man, so wonderful and gifted a being, *does not find his end in a cold, dark grave*. Atheists and agnostics there may be, but the singularities or foibles of individuals never weigh against the universal instincts of the race, and it is the belief of humanity at large in a world beyond the grave we have endeavoured to prove. Again, therefore, we broach the question, *How did this widespread belief in a future life originate?* There are rationalists who refuse to accept the truth of immortality because they say the same originated in man's faith in ghosts, or in the practice of ancestor worship, or in the universal belief in dreams. But all such explanations are puerile simply because the conceptions of the after-life held by all races represent the natural, ineradicable instinct of the soul, and not a colossal illusion. Our contention is that belief in a future state was derived from a revelation given to Adam and Eve by their Creator, and that this revelation continued through the ages, becoming broken up, perverted and corrupted among some peoples, while with other nations it retained its comparative purity in spite of transmission. Marcus Porcius Cato, the Roman philosopher who lived before Christ, gave the world his belief in another and better life to which every thoughtful noble soul can assent:

> It must be so—Plato, thou reasonest well:
> Else whence this pleasing hope, this fond desire,
> This longing after immortality?
> Of whence this secret dread, and inward horror
> Of falling into naught? Why shrinks the soul
> Back on herself and startles at destruction?
> 'Tis the divinity that stirs within us:
> 'Tis Heaven itself that points out an hereafter,
> And intimates Eternity to man.

The presence of all these instinctive widespread universal beliefs is a proof that as Paul told the heathen worshippers at Lystra, "Nevertheless He left not Himself without witness" (Acts 14: 17) although not until His coming was the truth as it is in Jesus made known.

CHAPTER THREE

The Progressive Revelation of Immortality

WHILE much can be learnt from History, Tradition, and Archaeology as to a universal belief in some sort of existence after death, our only authentic and final court of appeal is the Bible—the infallible revelation of the mind and purposes of God to man. To the Christian, there is the pre-eminent source of knowledge on any given matter, *What saith the Scriptures*. John Milton bids us remember:

> Yet some there be that by due steps aspire
> To lay their just hands on that golden key
> That opes the Palace of Eternity

it is in the Word of God alone that we have that golden key opening for us the revelation of the glorious Palace of Eternity. There are no speculations, colourful imaginations, maybe's or perhaps's in the Bible regarding the after life. Behind every statement we have Divine authority, and certainty of fulfilment. Arnold Bennett, a pronounced and brilliant agnostic of a past generation, gave vent to the dogmatic statement:

"I am convinced as I am of anything that we shall never know what death signifies and involves."

Having been dead for a few years now, Bennett knows only too well what his death signified and involves. This agnostic said *we shall never know*, but a greater than Bennett wrote, '*We know* that if our earthly house of this tabernacle were dissolved, *we have* a building of God, an house not made with hands, eternal in the heavens' (2 Cor. 5: 1). Thus the choice is between, *We shall never know* and *We know . . . we have*. Needless to say, we prefer the certainty of the Apostle to the doubt of the agnostic.

When men reject the Bible as their guide, and fail to seek the light of a Divine revelation on such a solemn theme as *The Hereafter*, how they grope in darkness! The unproved and unproven theory of Evolution has the tendency to present man as a self-evolved, self-sustained being, a highly-evolved animal who, like all other animals, moulders into dust at death, and becomes extinct. Homer, the traditional Greek epic poet of 850 B.C., expressed such extinction in his pathetic picture of the fading and falling autumn leaves, and then swept away by winter winds. Listen to the note of despair in this song of unbelief:

There is one steady star: and, dim from afar,
    Comes the solace that lies in its gleam;
There's the coffin nail's thrust; the brain is white dust;
    And the sleeping that knows no dream.

Poor solace this for those with a heart-hunger and a ceaseless longing for a fuller life beyond the seeming hopelessness of the grave. Another hopeless agnostic cry is just as tragic:

To thy dark chamber, Mother Earth, I come:
Prepare my dreamless bed for my last home;
Shut down the marble door,
And leave me; let me sleep;
But deep, deep;
Never to waken more.

God pity us if the grave is our last home! If death means oblivion, then we are of all men most miserable. How different is that luminous ray of light from the brain and heart of Ralph W. Emerson, the American poet and essayist. In one of his sunny-hearted letters to Thomas

Carlyle, he wrote: "What have we to do with old age? Our existence looks to me, more than ever, *initial*. We have come to see the ground and look at our materials and tools. Man serves his apprenticeship here for a noble vocation hereafter." Praise God! we have not been left as derelicts upon the ocean of uncertainty, because His Word has given us abundant proof of the truth that upon every pale bosom of those who walked with Him amid the shadows of earth we can lay the unwithering rose of Immortality—*Absent from the body—Present*, or *At Home, with the Lord*.

Commenting upon Paul's phrase about being, "at home with the Lord" (2 Cor. 5: 6–9), that saintly scholar the late Bishop Handley Moule says:

"The Heaven beyond death is Home. It is not only rest or refuge: it is nothing less than Home. And Home is more than a place of safety or of repose. It is the scene where our whole being is in sweet and vivid harmony with surroundings. To enter the unseen state, the Christian is not to totter out into the cold and void. It is to 'get Home' The Home will be indeed a circle of blessed fellowship, a place of inconceivable interchange of love and joy among its inhabitants. But the supreme bliss of it which will always spring up through everything else, and be first in everything, is this— we shall have 'got Home to the Lord'."

Give a man all of the world he asks for, and he is yet unsatisfied. He feels and knows that his nature is too large for this present scene of existence as Browning expresses it in *Pauline*:

> I cannot chain my soul; it will not rest
> In its clay prison, this most narrow sphere.
> It has strange powers, and feelings, and desires
> Which I cannot account for nor explain,
> But which I stifle not, being bound to trust
> All feelings equally, to hear all sides.
> Yet I cannot indulge them, and they live,
> Referring to some state of life unknown.

But the state of life beyond this narrow sphere is not altogether unknown. Still discontented, in spite of the accumulation of money, pleasure, honours and wisdom the man tormented with desires for complete satisfaction can turn to the Bible and hear and heed the voice of the Psalmist, "I shall be satisfied when I awake in Thy likeness". As we approach the Biblical revelation of our destiny there are two preliminary aspects we must briefly mention. The first is, that the Bible alone contains the original conception of Immortality, as previously suggested in our reference to the beliefs in non-Christian lands. Here, in Holy Writ, the portrayal of a future life is different from that to be found in profane literature because "holy men of old" were guided by the Divine Author of the Book in all they wrote.

As far as the Old Testament is concerned, the conception of Immortality may be somewhat dim and fragmentary, and that, for the most part, piety has its field in this world, and faith in its satisfaction in present relations to God. Further, there may be little in the form of a doctrine of the future life, but rather an emphasis on this present world rather than one to come. Nevertheless, what the Old Testament does say is, "something that was its own from the first, an independent doctrine, if doctrine it may be called, equally free from the gross and extraordinary ideas with which the hope of an after-existence was overlaid in some races, and from the refinements of philosophy by which it was misdirected in others". Rigidly excluded from its sacred pages are the ideas of extinction, annihilation, transmigration of souls and other extravagances so common to ancient heathen faiths and philosophies.

The second matter is that, as the Bible presents a progressive revelation, or a gradual unfolding of any doctrine, thus we expect in the full blaze of revelation the New Testament possesses a fuller conception of life after death than that to be found in the Old Testament. An inescapable law of Scripture in respect to revelation of a truth is that it proceeds by stages from the simple to the more advanced unfolding, from the rudimentary to the final. "First the blade, then the ear, then the full corn in the ear." To ancient Israel, revelation was a revelation in twilight, with the grave as the horizon. The Hebrew had a somewhat gloomy conception of Death in that it removed him from fellowship with the living here below, and likewise removed him, as he thought, from fellowship with God. Man passed into an underworld where all joy and hope ceased. But although the revelation was only partial it was sufficient for pious minds to rest in. They took some kind of a future life for granted as Salmond assures us:

The Essence of God

"That there is a Beyond of some form, is one of the things most obviously presupposed all through the Old Testament in the Pentateuch and the Book of Job not less than in the Prophets. But if they do not discuss the life after death in any detailed way it is because the Kingdom Conception filled their minds. The continual absorption with a new condition of things coming on earth. A King was coming and through Him a Kingdom."

Now let us examine some of the Old Testament passages replete with the truth and hope of Immortality, and discover how the saints of old not only endured as seeing Him Who is invisible but were upheld by a belief in the unseen and eternal world beyond this present world.

At the very beginning of the Bible we have a strong, unassailable evidence of Immortality in the majestic phrase, "In the beginning God", Who, because of His deathlessness is "the King-Immortal". After his creation, man based his unhesitating hope of a Beyond upon what they knew of the being of God. Man did not argue "Because of what I am I must be immortal". His argument was, "Because God is what He is, He will never allow me to perish". When God breathed into the nostrils of Adam, a part of God became Adam's, namely, eternal existence. True, Adam, because of his disobedience died physically —"In the day thou eatest thereof, thou shalt surely die"— but he received in the Divine breath life for evermore. As soon as a child is born and enters the world from the womb with physical life, it is likewise the recipient of a life without end. Is not this solemn fact resident in the declaration of Christ that God is not the God of the dead but of the living? (Exod. 3: 6; Mark 12: 25–27).

The phrase, "the breath of life" (Gen. 2: 7), can be translated, "the breath of *lives*". Man is different from an animal in that he has more than one life. A dog's life ends completely when it dies, but man lives on after death. Coming from the Immortal One, he bears the image of his Creator. The part of man that cannot be holden of death is that part God gave Adam of Himself when He graciously breathed into his nostrils. Thus, because He ever lives, we shall live also.

The Escape From Death

Enoch, the seventh from Adam, unlike all others before him, did not die. "He walked with God and he was not: for God took him" (Gen. 5: 24). "He was translated that he should not see death" (Heb. 11: 5, 6). Enoch's friends sought him, but he could not be found (Ps. 37: 36). Where did God take Enoch to, and to what sphere was Enoch, like Elijah (2 Kings 2: 11) translated? There can only be one answer to such a question, namely, God took both Enoch and Elijah from earth without dying to share His invisible state of existence in the Divine abode. Enoch walked with God and one day God said to His companion, "Why go back to your own home, come all the way this time with Me to My Eternal Home?" So he was missed from earth, for God had taken him to be with Himself. This was a foreshadow of the Master's promise, "Where I am, there shall ye be also" (John 14: 3).

The Gathering of the Elect

The expressions are often used of those who died "gathered to his people", "gathered to his fathers". At the death of the patriarch Abraham, it is said that, "he was gathered to his people" (Gen. 25: 8). Such a phrase does not mean that he was buried in the grave containing the dead bodies of his relatives but that he was reunited with them in Paradise. Abraham was buried in the lonely grave in the Cave of Machpelah, a great distance from the Ur of the Chaldees, where his people lay buried. Therefore, being "gathered to his people" means that he rejoined the spirits of his kindred in Eternity. When our Lord used the illustration of a homely gathering, "And shall sit down with Abraham, Isaac and Jacob", He suggested recognition, as well as a pleasant welcome and communion, in the unseen world.

The Patriarchal Hope

As he faced death in Egypt, Joseph said to his brethren, "Carry up my bones from hence", and it was left to Moses to fulfil the behest (Gen. 50: 26; Exod. 13: 19; Heb. 11: 22). Probably it was the hope of resurrection that prompted the great care of the Israelites for their dead, and which, therefore, led to the injunction of both Jacob and Joseph that the interment of their bones should be in the land of Promise. Was not Abraham's sacrifice of Isaac coupled with his faith in a resurrection? "By faith Abraham . . . offered up Isaac . . . accounting that God was able to raise up, even from the dead; whence also he did in a parable receive him back" (Heb. 11: 17–19).

The Witch of Endor

The narrative taken up with the desperation of Saul, the practice of the witch-medium and the reappearance of Samuel from the dead continues to be a happy hunting-ground for spiritualists or spiritists. Amid much our finite minds cannot explain in connection with this episode, one fact is evident, namely, that the Prophet Samuel after being dead for some time reappeared for a brief moment, and was recognized both by Saul and the Witch, proving, thereby, that although Samuel died physically he was still alive with an unmistakable identity. Furthermore, his answer to Saul revealed a concern in the affairs of earth as keen as ever, a mentality as vigorous as ever, and speech as clear and incisive as before his death.

With scathing sarcasm Rudyard Kipling denounced the wicked system:

> The road to En-dor is easy to tread
>   for mother or yearning wife,
> There, she is sure we shall meet with our dead
>   as they were even in life.
> Earth has not dreamed of the blessing in store
>   for the desolate hearts on the road to En-dor.
>
> Oh, the road to En-dor is the oldest road
>   and the craziest road of all!
> Straight it runs to the witch's abode
>   as it did in the days of Saul;
> And nothing has changed of the sorrow in store
>   for such as go down the road to En-dor.

The Translation of Elijah

As already indicated both Enoch and Elijah escaped physical death and went straight into the immediate abode of God (2 Kings 2). At the transfiguration of Christ (Matt. 17: 1–8), the translated Elijah reappeared along with Moses on the mount, to converse with Christ about His coming death on the Cross. Peter, although he had never seen the Old Testament patriarchs in the flesh, immediately recognized and desired them to continue their reappearance on the earth. If this narrative does not teach the continuity of life after this life, as well as the full consciousness of the departed, then language has no meaning.

The Question of Job

Probably the sublime *Book of Job* is the oldest in the world, going back before Moses wrote *Genesis*. If this is so, then we here have the first expression of the never-ending problem of "man's destiny and God's ways with men here on earth", as Carlyle expresses it in his "Heroes and Hero Worship". Because this earliest of all Old Testament books contains a few peaks of the mountain range of Immortality, Job reflects the common belief of same in the early twilight of the human race. In his answer to Bildad Job discoursed on Immortality in a passage so laden with the certainty of Resurrection (14: 7–17). Within such is a most pertinent question: "If a man die, shall he live again?" (14: 14). Taken in its context, this is not so much a question of uncertainty but rather an affirmation, a confession of Job's faith that death did not end all. A slight change in the order of the question can more clearly express Job's thought: "If a man die, he *shall* live, or live again."

Yet taken as a question, it is one of perennial interest and likewise a most pressing one, for if man does not live on beyond the tomb then he is of all men most miserable. Further, "if the dead rise not, then is not Christ raised" (1 Cor. 15: 16). Some, there are, who find it convenient to deny existence after death because if the grave ends all and there is no final reckoning then why concern ourselves about how we live on the earth or whether there be a God in Heaven to please and glorify? We can eat, drink, abandon ourselves to the flesh if death on the morrow means oblivion. But Job, out of the agony of his heart, assures us of Immortality:

"As for me I know that my Vindicator liveth, and at last He will stand up upon the earth: and after my skin hath been thus destroyed, yet from my flesh shall I see God, Whom I, even I, shall see for myself, and mine eyes shall behold Him, and not as a stranger" (19: 25–27).

Could anything be more emphatic than this prophetic voice, *I shall see God?* Living in the dawn of revelation, there was much that was dark to Job's mind, but of this the patriarch was certain that after waiting for a time like a sentinel at his post he expected to hear and answer his Captain's call to present himself in His presence.

The Musings of David

More than any other Old Testament writer, David lived in the realm of certainty regarding the glorious future once the numbering of his days on earth was finished. When his child by Bathsheba died, King David surprised the mourners by saying, "I will go to him, but he will not return to me" (2 Sam. 12: 23). The bereaved father had no doubt in the continued existence of his infant son beyond death; and the expected reunion with the child, David, with his intense, emotional nature dearly loved, along with identity and recognition are directly implied in David's beautiful expression. Principal Garvie wrote that "Human affection is the measure of its intensity, elevation and purity demands continuance, challenges death's right to end the loving fellowship of kindred souls". Tennyson offers us the same line of reason in his *In Memoriam*. The poet felt that his deep love for another would not have been called into being simply to be mocked by death. The deep love binding Tennyson and young Hallam together compelled the poet to declare his belief that his much-loved companion lived, and so concludes his remarkable poem:

> Dear heavenly friend, that canst not die;
> Mine, mine, forever, ever mine . . .
> Far off thou art, but ever nigh;
> I have thee still, and I rejoice;
> I prosper, circled with thy voice;
> I shall not lose thee tho' I die.

All through *The Psalms* hope springs eternal and the foregleams of a conscious existence in the House of the Lord forever are numerous. Here are a few passages that speak for themselves:

"My flesh also shall rest in hope. For Thou wilt not leave my soul in the grave; neither wilt Thou suffer Thine Holy One to see corruption. . . . At Thy right hand there are pleasures for evermore" (Psalm 16: 9–11).

Luke cites this portion as a prophecy of the Resurrection of Christ (Acts 2: 24–31), as, of course, it was. But what David wrote is likewise true of every born-again believer: Death is only a transition into the presence of God where the fulness of joy is to be experienced.

> There is a heritage of joy,
>   That yet I must not see.
> The Hand that bled to make it mine,
>   Is keeping it for me.

The consummation of the believer's satisfaction can be found in David's prayer, "As for me, I will behold Thy face in righteousness, I shall be satisfied, when I awake, in Thy likeness" (Psalm 17: 15). Here we have the same high, exultant assurance of an after-life, with its complete identification with the Lord of Glory. When Charles Wesley came to die his last words were, "I shall be satisfied with Thy likeness; satisfied, satisfied, SATISFIED!" Evan H.

Hopkins composed the prayer-hymn multitudes still offer:

> Work on, then, Lord, till on my soul
>   Eternal light shall break,
> And, in Thy likeness perfected,
>   I *satisfied* shall wake.

Then David uses the phrase "The House of the Lord", in a double way. His one desire was "to dwell in the house of the Lord all the days of his life, to behold the beauty of the Lord, and to enquire in His temple" (Psalm 27: 4). The sanctuary built by man was to the Psalmist, God's house or temple in which he loved to worship. But in David's Psalm of the Shepherd, he concludes with a declaration and a determination, "Surely goodness and mercy shall follow me *all the days of my life*," and when he came to the end of his earthly pilgrimage, he knew that he would dwell in the house of the Lord *for ever* (Psalm 23: 6), where he would be able perfectly to worship in the beauty of holiness.

A further word of assurance that although dust returns to dust, the believer lives on can be gathered from the assertion: "But God will redeem my soul from the power of the grave: for He shall receive me. Selah"—think of that! (Psalm 49: 14–15). That the Lord receives the spirit of the believer at death is emphasized by Stephen's dying prayer:

> "Lord Jesus, receive my spirit" (Acts 7: 59).

Asaph, another Psalmist, likewise gave us a passage pregnant with the hope of Resurrection. Although pressed by the dark enigmas of existence here below, with the terror of unlooked-for dangers threatening life, faith had its forecast and companionship with God incapable of cancellation by death. Think of this word we can hide in our heart as we linger amid the shadows:

"Thou shalt guide me with Thy counsel, and afterward receive me to glory. Whom have I in Heaven but Thee? and there is none upon earth that I desire beside Thee . . . God . . . is my portion forever" (Psalm 73 : 24–26).

Solomon, the illustrious son of David, also believed in the existence of life after death. *Ecclesiastes* may strike the low level ideally or spiritually in Solomon's writings, but although he wrote as "a jaded critic worn dull with his successive passionate indulgences", yet even here we have the incidental recognition after death. Previously, in dealing with the instinct in man regarding Immortality, we drew attention to the Revised Translation of Eccles. 3: 11, "He hath set Eternity in their heart". We can but add that as the Eternal One, God in creating man made him a sharer of His Eternity. That Solomon believed the sky to be his goal can be gathered from the remarkable description he gives us of Death and its issue. "The dust shall return to the earth as it was and the spirit shall return unto God, who gave it" (Eccles. 12 : 7), hence the funeral formula *Ashes to ashes, dust to dust*. Here we have the dissolution of the body which belongs to nature. "Every particle of which it was composed had been drawn from her stores, and back to Nature every particle returns. It was borrowed only; it is repaid; no part is lost. Hence the euphemism by which we seek to soften the word *death*, by saying that such and such a one has "paid the debt of Nature". "Once the spirit has departed, Nature and we are quits; we can defraud her, she will receive her own to the exacted tittle". Von Stalberg puts it:

> Mother Earth she gathers all
> Under her bosom, great and small;
> O, could we look into her face,
> We should not shrink from her embrace.

As the body returns to its natural home, likewise the spirit returns to its natural element, even to God Himself. Bodies go to the dust of the earth to which they originally belonged but their tenants, our spirits, return to Him Who, by His own creative act, imparted them to men.

Isaiah, the evangelical Prophet, goes further than any other Old Testament writer in the declaration of the belief that Immortality would be realized by Resurrection. In an exultant climax of victory over all foes, Isaiah represents Death as abolished. Think of these glimpses he gives us:

A World without Tears

"He hath swallowed up death for ever; and the Lord God will wipe away tears from off all faces; and the reproach of His people will He take away from off all the earth: for Jehovah hath spoken it" (25 : 8).

The certainty of Heaven as a tearless world can be found in the latter phrase, *Jehovah hath spoken it*. Isaiah's language is laid hold of both by Paul and John to declare Christ's grand victory and ringing cry of triumph over death (see 1 Cor. 15: 56–57; Rev. 7: 17; 21: 4).

Resurrection of Dust Dwellers

"The dead shall live, thy dead bodies shall arise. Awake and sing, ye that dwell in the dust; for the dew of God is a life-giving dust, and the earth shall cast forth her dead" (6: 19, S. D. Gordon paraphrase).

Here, speaking as the national leader, Isaiah proclaims that God will perform the impossible. As Oehler states it in his *Theology of the Old Testament*, "That the power of God *can*, against all human thought, re-animate the dead is the general idea of the passage from which consequently the Life of a literal resurrection of the dead can be inferred." The vision and valley of dry bones likewise expresses Israel's hope (Ezek. 37: 1–10).

The Two Destinies

"Many that sleep in the dust of the earth shall awake, some to everlasting life, and some to shame and everlasting contempt. And they that are wise shall shine as the brightness of the firmament; and they that turn many to righteousness as the stars for ever and ever" (Daniel 12 : 2, 3).

Is this not the most definite, most literal, and the largest expression of the hope of a resurrection in the Old Testament? Here we have, so clearly defined, the resurrection of both the just and unjust as a resurrection with destined moral issues. The special feature of interest in this passage is that it contains the first mention of the resurrection of the wicked as of the just, more fully dealt with in New Testament Scriptures. Daniel received from God the beautiful promise of his own share in the resurrection of the just, "Thou shalt die, but when these events occur thou shalt be living and be in thine allotted place" (12 : 13).

Two further passages from the Minor Prophets suffice to prove that no matter how dimly or obscurely Old Testament saints understood the fact of Immortality in the twilight of Revelation, none is said or shown forbidding the hope and universal expectation of life beyond the grave. Saints of old could have subscribed to *The Apostle's Creed*: "I believe in the resurrection of the body and the life everlasting." Listen to the assertion of Hosea, whose style as a writer is not only abrupt but remarkably metaphorical and figurative:

"After two days will He revive us : in the third day He will raise us up, and we shall live in His sight" (6 : 2).
". . . I will ransom them from the graves; I will redeem them from death : O death, I will be thy plagues; O grave, I will be thy destruction : repentance shall be hid from Mine eyes" (13 : 14; 1 Cor. 15 : 55).

The Full Radiance of Revelation

What is partially concealed in the Old Testament is fully revealed in the New Testament where proofs of Immortality glitter on almost every page. Between the two parts of the Bible known as the Inter-Testament Period, we have a silence of some 400 years, yet as Salmond reminds us, "Between the period when the last of the Old Testament prophets spoke and the Christian era opened, there had been a remarkable development of belief. . . . Along with this, some of the familiar Old Testament lines had undergone a change of meaning, and new modes of speech had been introduced." *The Talmud* proves this for it teaches that the purpose of life here on earth is the preparation of ourselves for the life hereafter:

> "This world is to be likened to the porch, the world to come unto the palace. Prepare thyself in the porch that thou mayest be worthy to enter the palace."

A noticeable feature of the New Testament fuller revelation of the Hereafter is the way it confirms, as well as elaborates, the faith of Old Testament saints. Our Lord quoted the revelation given to Moses when, in describing the life of those in Heaven, He spoke of God as being the God, not of the dead, but of the living (Exod. 3: 6; Mark 12: 25–27). Paul, in extending the doctrines of a resurrection of the dead, affirmed that such was the Life of Israel, and of the Pharisees who came into being during the period between the Old and New Testaments (Acts 23: 6; 26: 6–8). From the *Epistle to the Hebrews*, we find how the Hebrew saints in the Old Testament were commended for the bright hope beyond this life that sustained them amid their trials. Abraham "looked for a city which hath foundations, whose builder and maker is God". Multitudes of the saints, conscious that they were only strangers and pilgrims here on earth, were upheld by the vision of a better, heavenly country God had prepared for them. Moses gladly sacrificed so much of the profit and pleasure gained in Egypt because he "looked for the recompence of reward". Others willingly endured torture, trials and tribulations "that they might obtain a better resurrection" (Heb. 11: 10; 11: 13, 14, 26, 35). The faith of the ancient Hebrews in life and immortality was brought to fuller light by the Gospel (2 Tim. 1: 10).

The more radiant revelation of another life was not given to satisfy mere curiosity, neither does it answer all the questions of head and heart. The veil on the unseen is not completely removed but lifted sufficiently to confirm faith in the glorious inheritance of the saints. When the Bible speaks of Heaven, it generally uses expressive imagery, and is always careful to bring the future and the present into right focus. While a Book of both worlds, its emphasis is upon the responsibilities of the life that now is, rather than that which is to come. As it has been expressed:

> "The Bible teaches human life on its ideal and practical side; it teaches man has this below. It teaches the most perfect secularism, using that word in its true sense. It is a book for this world. If its precepts were followed, our World would become a paradise. . . . But the Bible is also a book of the other world as well as of this."

Much of the teaching of this other world came from Christ Who never sought to offer proofs of the certainty of a future existence, but presupposed that existence. He dispelled the clouds so that men could know more of the reality of Heaven—and Hell. He did not originate Immortality, either by His teaching or His own resurrection from the grave. He brought the unseen to light, just as a telescope brings to sight stars hitherto unseen by the naked, unaided eye. Writing on our Lord's own doctrine of the world beyond, Professor James Stalker says that:

> "It is too fresh and original to have been obtained secondhand. He speaks as one who has been there, and the statement of the New Testament is literally true, that He brought life and immortality to light by the Gospel."

In parable, precept and promise Christ taught the realities of the unseen, eternal world. As Canon Knox Little summarizes it:

"Our Lord revealed it—

By His Example, by the manner in which He subordinated the claims of this present world to the thought of a life beyond:

By the Whole Tenor of His Teaching, the precepts of which require for their adequate fulfilment a life beyond the narrow boundary of time:

By direct Statement—'God, not the God of the dead but of the living'—'Many mansions'—'Abraham's bosom'—'Shining forth as the righteous in their Father's Kingdom'. He revealed it, and guaranteed the truth of His Godhead, and, therefore, His right to reveal, by the stupendous miracle of the Resurrection. He carried on His revelation by His Ascension into Glory and by the coming of the Holy Spirit."

Because He was "The Truth" (John 14: 6), all He taught in the Parable of the Virgins, in the story of Dives and Lazarus, in His miracles of raising the dead, in His teaching on His Second Advent, was in harmony with His character. Paul in his *Magna Carta* of the Resurrection (1 Cor. 15), declares the Lord's resurrection to be the pledge and pattern of our resurrection from the dead. Job's question, "If a man die, shall he live again?" is answered by the empty grave of Jesus, Who said, "Because I live, ye shall live also" (John 14: 19; Rom. 8: 11). For years, men argued about the possibility of there being a new world out yonder towards the west, but it was only after Christopher Columbus sailed out and discovered the unknown, that he could return and say, "There is a land out yonder. I have been there. Look, here are some of its riches!" Jesus lived before He was born. His abode from Eternity had been with the Father. He came from Heaven. But as our heavenly Columbus, He travelled back there by the way of a grave, and returned to tell His own of "the land of pure delight, where saints immortal reign".

It is not true to speak of the country on the other side of death as one from which no traveller has returned to describe its splendour. Lazarus and the others raised from the dead during our Lord's life came back, and although we have no record of theirs of what they experienced, our Lord's testimony is more than sufficient. Dr. Ross H. Stover, of Philadelphia, was advertised to give a series of lectures on "What do We Know about Life After Death?" A man, invited to the lectures by a friend, said, "What does he know about life after death? Has he ever been there?" Told of this, Dr. Stover replied, "No, I have never been there. But I have a very dear Friend who has been there—Jesus Christ, the risen Lord, and I am simply repeating what this dear Friend told me."

Believing all that Jesus taught of the Father's home above, multitudes of saints and martyrs died triumphant, knowing that on the other side of the river of death the Deathless One would be waiting to welcome them home.

"We bow our heads at going out, we think,
  And enter straight another golden chamber of the King's
  Larger than this we leave, and lovelier."

As they were taught of the Lord, and instructed by the Holy Spirit, the Apostles were no less definite and explicit in their witness to the resurrection of the dead, and of the glory beyond, as the Lord they loved and followed. The Apostles one and all taught what Christ had revealed, and now the whole Church throughout the world, however externally divided through human frailties, still, as God's family, proclaims with one living voice in the catholic creeds, "I believe in the resurrection of the body, the life everlasting, the life of the world to come".

If space allowed, it would be profitable to gather out from *The Acts*, and all *The Epistles*, the contribution of each writer to the revelation of the future. From Genesis to Revelation, the existence and nature of God bespeak our Immortality. The closing verses of the Bible conclude the unfolding of the progressive revelation as to the coming bliss of the redeemed as Jesus returns to gather them unto Himself. It is interesting to note some of the expressive figures used of our transition. Both Christ and the Apostles referred to Death as *Sleep*:

> "Our friend Lazarus sleepeth" (John 11 : 11).
> "Them that sleep in Jesus" (1 Thess. 4 : 14).

At the outset, it is essential to bear in mind that *Sleep* is only used of the body, never of the spirit part of man. There are those who erroneously teach that when a saint dies—*he dies*: that as his body perishes, he, himself, passes into a condition of unconsciousness or sleep until the last Judgment, and that for the sinner there is nothing but complete annihilation at death. The body of the believer is the only part of him that sleeps in the dust of the earth until the Lord's Return when all who died in Him are raised in His likeness.

Sleep brings rest to man's body, and so does death to the believer's body. The ancient Christians called their cemeteries *Cubicula*, or "sleeping places". Sleep indicates the absence of fear, as well as a condition of repose. Sleep brings rest to the body, just as death does, more extensively. Our death, then, is nothing but a long sleep, with the grave as a quiet resting place. It was Martin Luther who said that, "A man who lies asleep is much like one who is dead. Therefore the ancient sages declared that *sleep is the brother of death*". An old English author says, "Sleep is Death's youngest brother, and so like him, that I never dare trust him without my prayers". While the body reposes in the grave, the spirit—the person himself— is at rest with the Lord, because the repose of the spirit does not take the form of unconsciousness. There is the continuity of memory and activity after death. The spirit, absent from the body, is present with the Lord.

Article XL of the Forty-two Articles of The Church of
England, issued during the reign of Edward VI, states
briefly and clearly: "The souls of them that depart this
life do neither die with the bodies nor sleep idly. They
which say that the souls of such as depart hence do sleep,
being without all sense, feeling, or perceiving, until the
Day of Judgment . . . do utterly dissent from the right
belief declared to us in Holy Scriptures."

Death, even for a believer, may not lose its fearful
countenance, but for him the fear of death can be swallowed up in the certainty of a glorious life beyond. At
peace with God, he has no dread of something after death
as suggested in the famous lines:

> To die, to sleep;
> To sleep; perchance to dream; ay there's the rub:
> For in that sleep of death what dreams may come
> When we have shuffled off the mortal coil,
> Must give us pause . . .
> . . . The dread of something after death,
> The undiscovered country, from whose bourne
> No traveller returns, puzzles the will
> And makes us rather bear those ills we have
> Than fly to others that we know not of.

Paul also thought of death as a pulling up of the anchor
and setting sail, for this is what *departure* meant. "The
time of my departure is at hand" (2 Tim. 4: 6; Phil. 1:
23; see 2 Peter 1: 14). Here, on earth, we are anchored to
physical and material possessions, but at death we leave
these and sail for the heavenly port. "The time of my
spirit's release from the body is at hand and I will soon be
free," is the translation in *The Amplified Bible* of Paul's
announcement of his immediate death. Death is a departure from material possessions whether few or many, and
we leave the world as naked as we entered it. Sometimes,
when a person dies, we say, "How much did he leave?"
Why, he left all, for nothing is retained but character. It

is said that Alexander the Great requested that he might be buried with his hand *open* outside his coffin, indicating that he left the world as empty as he came into it. Death is also a departure from earthly honours whether scholastic, social, or political, for it removes us from the praise, as well as the blame of men. The only honour we can carry with us at our departure is that of a life lived nobly and well in the service of Christ.

At the funeral of Dr. John Mason Neale, of whom Archbishop Trench said, "He is the most profoundly learned hymnologist of our Church", his friends sang a special favourite of his, the first verse of which reads:

> Safe home, safe home, in port!
> Rent cordage, shattered deck,
> Torn sails, provisions short,
> And only not a wreck;
> But oh! the joy upon the shore,
> To tell our voyage—perils o'er!

A further expression, similar to "Departure" is *Decease*. "After my decease" (2 Peter 1: 15). "Spake of His decease" (Luke 9: 31). This term means "a going out" or an "exodus". The second book of the Bible is named *Exodus* because it records the going out of Israel from Egypt. Out, the people went, from bondage into liberty, out of a land of sorrow and affliction and need into a land flowing with milk and honey. In like manner "death" is a way out from the partial to the perfect. Not out of life into oblivion, but out from all the trammelling influences of the flesh into the Land of Promise—out into glory where the Divine plan for each of us will be fully realized. Even Victor Hugo, the renowned French novelist and poet, wrote these memorable words expressing what his *decease* would mean:

'For half a century I have been writing my thoughts in history, prose, verse, philosophy, drama, romance, tradition, satire, ode and song. I have tried all, but I feel that I have not said the thousandth part of what is in me. When I go down to my grave, I can say, like so many others, 'I have finished my day's work'; but I cannot say I have finished my life. My day's work will begin again the next morning. The tomb is not a blind alley; it is a thoroughfare; it closes in the twilight, to open with the dawn."

Another Pauline figure of "Death" is that of a *Removal* in which a tent is exchanged for a house. "If the earthly house of our tent be taken down, we have from God a building, a house not made with hands, eternal in the heavens" (2 Cor. 5: 1).

John Oxenham must have had the idea of Death as the striking of a tent when he wrote:

> Fold up the tent! the sun is in the west;
> This house was only lent
> For my apprenticement,
> And God knows best.
>
> Fold up the tent!
> Its slack ropes all undone,
> Its pole all broken, and its cover rent,
> Its work is done.

Life below is a pilgrimage, with the temporary abode of a fragile tent. Here we have no permanent residence, we seek one to come, and Death will be the pulling up of the tent pegs, the rolling up of the canvas and a journey into an abiding place above.

> Here in the body pent
> Absent from Him I roam,
> Yet nightly pitch my moving tent
> A day's march nearer Home.

Professor Wm. Clow says that, "Every reader of the New Testament is disconcerted by the contrast between the expectancy and desire of the Primitive Church and the bewilderment and shrinking of Christian men today.

44

Stephen saw Heaven opened; Paul longs to depart and be with Christ; Peter exults in an 'inheritance incorruptible, undefiled, and that fadeth not away'. The early believers might be pictured as looking stedfastly up into Heaven. Even a generation or two ago, devout men and women died with a psalm of desire on their lips. We still read, beside the bier of the dead, the wondrous words which proclaim the blessed resurrection. But, for most men the veil of sense hangs very darkly between. They have passed into a silent agnosticism. 'It does not yet appear what we shall be,' is the only sentence which receives the assent of many minds. But we have not so learned Christ! He has torn the mask away from the cruel face of death; has robbed it of its power to smite us with fear; has caused us to embrace death as our friend."

The Christian view of Death is totally different from the conception of those who, lacking the knowledge of Scripture, speak of The Great Beyond, The Unknown, The Unexplored Land, A Leap in the Dark. To the true believer, Death is the passing out of one life in which its purpose is probation, and whose distinction is the opportunity of attaining a higher and nobler life; it is an exodus from the wilderness of sin and sorrow into a land of fuller energy, happier fellowship, pure joy and perfect peace; it is a swift passage to a life with Christ for evermore; it is a gate into the Holy City, a quick journey home. No wonder the death of saints is so precious in the sight of the Lord. For them, death has lost its sting and the grave its victory.

Added to the witness of Christ and of His Apostles to the reality of Immortality, are the testimonies of saints all down the ages who received the full noontide of truth as to the life beyond. Death-bed utterances reveal a hope divinely implanted in the human heart, that when the heart ceases to beat, that that is not the end. Dante, the great Italian poet, in an hour of grief could write, "Thus I believe, thus I affirm, thus I am certain it is, that from this life I shall pass to another better." Robert Browning indicated the ground and source of Dante's faith, as well as his own, when he wrote in his wife's New Testament the Italian poet's testimony.

When Sir William Russell reached the scaffold on which he was to die, he took his watch and handing it to the physician who waited upon him said, "Will you kindly take my timepiece and keep it? I have no more use for it; I am now dealing with *Eternity*".

Another testimony by one about to die on the scaffold, prayed:

> "Lord, I am coming as fast as I can. I know I must pass through the shadow of death before I come to see Thee. But that is only *umbra mortis*, a shadow of death, a little darkness upon nature, since Thou, Lord, by Thy goodness, hast broken the jaws and the power of death."

A friend said to the renowned preacher, Frederick Denison Maurice, as he came to die, "You have preached your last sermon." "Aye," he replied, "but only my last sermon in *this* life." As John Newton neared his end, he said, "I am still in the land of the dying; I shall be in the land of the living soon." The dying words of the famous Earl Shaftesbury were, "I am touching the Hem of His garment". When Thomas Fuller, the English divine, came to his last moments he said to his nephew, James Cuthbert: "Good-night, James—but it will soon be morning!" In her extreme old age Anna L. Barbauld wrote the following stanza, which the poet Rogers regarded as one of the finest verses in English literature. Henry Crabb Robinson repeated it to Wordsworth and heard him say: "I am not in the habit of grudging people their good things, but I wish I had written those lines." Here they are:

> Life! we have been long together,
> Through pleasant and through cloudy weather,
> 'Tis hard to part when friends are dear,
> Perhaps 'twill cost a sigh, a tear;

> Then steal away; give little warning;
> Choose thine own time.
> Say not, *Good-Night!* but in some brighter clime,
> Bid me, *Good-Morning!*

The saints of the early Church, while they did not ignore the fact of death, never spoke of it as something to expect and cast a halo about it. To them, it was an enemy, the last enemy, to be destroyed. Nor did they dwell very much on Heaven as the consummation of their pilgrimage. They thought of the true Church as being in Heaven already. Had she not been raised up with Christ and made to sit with Him in heavenly places? (Ephes. 2: 6). Is not her warfare against spiritual hosts of wickedness in the heavenlies? (Ephes. 6: 12). Is not her citizenship already in Heaven? (Phil. 3: 20). Thus, to New Testament believers Heaven was not so much in the future, as in the present. True, though it is, that a few glimpses of the blissful hereafter were granted them, not to satisfy any curiosity about the life beyond, but to show and help them to live rightly here and now, so as those who *are* citizens of the commonwealth which is Heaven we, too, should be found perfecting holiness in the fear of the Lord.

CHAPTER FOUR

The Location of the Saints' Everlasting Rest

Sir John Suckling (1609 to 1642) wrote:

'Tis expectation makes a blessing dear;
Heaven were not Heaven, if we knew what it were.

While we do not know all we would like to regarding the whereabouts of Heaven and all it represents, enough has been revealed to feed our expectation. With our finite, limited faculties it is impossible fully to comprehend all that is meant by *Heaven*. Of this fact we can be certain, however, that as the Bible is the only authentic revelation of the final destiny of man, sufficient knowledge of the same can be found within its sacred pages. The inspired writers have given us a partial unfolding of the future in allegory and gorgeous vision, piling up images of things we can see, like precious and beautiful thrones and crowns and gates of pearl and golden streets all of which is reserved only for those saved by grace and, therefore, heirs of the glory yet to be revealed. The final goal of the redeemed, the grand and glad finale of the history of all who are Christ's, and the end of God's loving purpose and the realization of the eternal thought in His mind from creation, is the presence of His Church with Him throughout Eternity.

If we accept the doctrine of a future life as taught by Christ, Prophets and Apostles, then we must have some sphere in which to live such a life. Certain, as He was, of the reality of Heaven, seeing He had lived there before He was born a child in Bethlehem, Christ never told His disciples where it was located. When He addressed them in the upper chamber, He did not give them an elaborate description of the position in which Heaven lay, but simply comforted their hearts by assuring them that there was such a place in His Father's home, and that He was specially going away to prepare it for them. Any further explanation of the vast expanse and wondrous details of such a preparation would have been beyond their comprehension to grasp. So Christ did not elaborate upon *where* Heaven was, but in simple language assured those plain, earnest but unlettered men what they could grasp, namely, the blessed reality of the Home beyond.

An examination of the terms used in connection with Heaven may prove profitable at this point. Cosmologically, it was one of the two great divisions of the universe. "In the beginning God created the heaven and the earth" (Gen. 1: 1; Ezek. 32: 7–8). We have heaven, earth, and water under the earth (Exod. 20: 4). In the visible heavens there are the stars and planets (Gen. 1: 14–17). Heaven and Earth, as terms, exclude one another, but together constitute the universe of God (Gen. 2: 1; Matt. 5: 18; 1 Cor. 8: 5). God, as the Most High, is "possessor of heaven and earth" (Gen. 14: 19–22), and Jesus recognized His Father as "Lord of heaven and earth" (Matt. 11: 25). The original simple distribution of all things in the universe under the phrase "heaven and earth" is sometimes expanded as, for instance, by John in his description, "the heaven and the earth and the sea and the fountains of water" (Rev. 14: 7). The vast expanse above and around our earth is phenomenally like one of the ancient mirrors made of firm molten polished metal. "Spread out . . . strong . . . as a molten looking glass" (Gen. 1: 16; Job 37: 18; Isa. 44: 24). *Heaven* is used of the surrounding air wherein "the fowls of heaven fly" (Gen. 1: 20, 26). From it, rain and hail fall (Deut. 11: 11). "I will make your heaven as iron", that is "your sky hard yielding no rain" (Lev. 26: 19). "The four corners of heaven" and "the circuit of heaven" (Job 22: 14; Jerm. 49: 36) are phrases referring to the atmospheric heaven.

The Jews divided the heavens into seven strata. *Seven* was a figure the Jews found irresistible, and so "the doctrine of seven Heavens was prevalent in Judaism before and after the time of Christ". *The Talmud* actually names these arbitrary and forced Heavens. Certainly, the immensity of Heaven may suggest to the beholder a plurality of spheres behind the firmament, hence the multiplication, "The Heaven, and the Heaven of Heavens" (Deut. 10: 14; 1 Kings 8: 27). Scripture, however, speaks of only three Heavens, with God's presence, not confined to any one region, but as the Creator of the entire universe, everywhere at the same time. Paul was caught up to "the third heaven" which he also called "Paradise" (2 Cor. 12: 1–4). This is "the Heaven of heavens", the residence of God, of Christ, the Angelic Host, and the blessed; the true palace of God, entirely separated from the alterations and changes of the lower worlds. Here is "the habitation of His holiness, the place where His honour dwells". The other two Heavens are:

The Firmament, with its stars and planets. "When I consider the Heavens . . . the moon, and the stars" (Psalm 8: 3).

The Aerial Heaven, where the birds fly, the winds blow, and the showers are formed. "Windows of heaven were opened" (Gen. 7: 11), represents the atmosphere on which the clouds float and out of which rain comes. Malachi uses the same phrase, figuratively, to describe the revival blessing from the Lord (3: 10). Closed heavens indicate drought, both materially and spiritually (James 5: 17, 18; Psalm 66: 18).

The phrase, "The heaven of heavens", is a Hebraism for "the highest heaven" (Deut. 10: 14; Pss. 68: 33; 148: 4), and represents the heavens *par excellence*, and agrees with the fuller phrase, "the heaven and the heaven of heavens", which was the sphere Paul reached when he was caught up to after passing through the first heaven—the air; the second heaven—the sky of the stars (2 Cor. 12: 2). Christ was "made higher than the heavens" and passed through the heavens, namely, the aerial heaven and the starry heaven (Ephes. 4: 10; Heb. 4: 14; 7: 26). He passed through the outer veils and then through the veil into the holy of holies, or the immediate presence of God. "The height of heaven" (1 Kings 8: 27) whose top can be reached. Here we have an unusual hyperbole expressing a great height (Deut. 1: 28; 9: 1). As a term, *Heavens* is used to describe the powerful providence of God (Dan. 4: 26)—that which is good and honourable (Luke 15: 18) —political or ecclesiastical government (Isa. 13: 13; Haggai 2: 6, 21). The aerial and starry heavens are to pass away or burn up (2 Peter 3: 7, 10), and in their place will appear the new heavens and earth. *Heaven*, God's abode, is stable and permanent; but the universe is to be purified, as the result of a cosmic upheaval (Isa. 34: 4–5; 65: 17; 66: 22; Rev. 6: 12–14).

"The heavens do rule" and "The kingdom of the heavens" (Dan. 2: 44; 4: 26), stand for the kingdom-rule of God, the sphere from which He governs—His seat of authority and power. There must be a place where God is present in an especial sense, from which He manifests Himself as ruling, judging, and above all, communicating grace and glory. Thus as "the God of Heaven" He sits on His throne and rules, and from such looks down on man (Gen. 24: 7; Psalms 2: 4; 11: 4; Isa. 66: 1; Jonah 1: 9; Rev. 11: 13; 16: 11). Various other designations of God's holy habitation all go to prove it to be a place. For instance, Heaven is represented as a *Building* or Mansion of God in which His love is sovereign (John 14: 2; 2 Cor. 5: 1). As a building its vault rests upon foundations and pillars (2 Sam. 22: 8); and an entrance gate (Gen. 28: 17); and windows opened for the gifts of God to benefit the earth (Gen. 7: 11; 2 Kings 7: 2; Mal. 3: 10).

Heaven is also likened to a *Temple*, in which God's excellent glory is revealed in the most conspicuous manner —a sacred Mansion of light, joy and glory. Then there will be no separate temple, for the whole of Heaven is one vast temple, finding its centre in the Lord God Almighty and the Lamb, Who are the temple to each and all the king-priests reigning and serving there. "There shall be no temple therein" (Rev. 21: 22), for the whole shall be perfectly consecrated to God. Another description of Heaven is that of a *City*, in which all "the citizens live a divinely co-operative social life"—a city without traffic problems, crooked councillors, or shame of any kind (Heb. 11: 10, 16; 12: 22; Rev. 21: 23–26; 22: 14). Heaven is also spoken of as a *Country*, of exquisite beauty and bountiful in provision; an *Inheritance* incorruptible, undisfigured of any grave; undefiled, uncontaminated by any stain of sin; unfading, untouched by any blight of change (Heb. 11: 16; Acts 20: 32; 1 Peter 1: 4). *The Amplified Bible* translates the passage dealing with those in search of a fatherland and often homesick for the country from which they emigrate as, "yearning for and aspiring to a better and more desirable country, that is, a heavenly one". Americans love to sing, "My Country 'tis of thee", but Heaven will far outstrip even America with all its resources and riches.

Where is the country anyone of us would want to live in for ever? Where is there a country without sin, crime, lawlessness, bloodshed, disease, death, sorrow and heartache? Heaven is a country in which there is the absence of all that is common to any land for in God's country there are no barriers, no walls or curtains to divide; no race barrier, no soldiers because there are no wars; no policemen because there is no crime or sin, no undertakers because there are no graves; no physicians because germs. fevers, pestilences, diseases are unknown; no thieves because there is no darkness. Who would not yearn for this better and more desirable country in which there are no separations, no broken homes, no drunkards, no prisons, no hospitals, no beggars, no persons who are blind, deaf, dumb or destitute? What a country! Are you not home-sick for Heaven?

Jesus spoke of Heaven as His *Father's House* or as *The Twentieth Century New Testament* renders the passage:

"In My Father's Home there are many dwellings" (John 14 : 2).

This is "The House of the Lord", David longed to live in for ever (Ps. 23 : 6), and which, with its many places of abode, will be as commodious as it will be beautiful. In London, quite near to Buckingham Palace, there are what are known as *Grace and Favour Apartments*, a row of houses or flats which the reigning Sovereign can allo-cate to those who have been conspicuous in national life, and where they can live rent free. Bless God, all the dwell-ing-places in the Father's home are associated with "Grace and Favour"—nothing will be ours by human merit, only because of God's grace and favour. Emphasis here is surely on the Head of the Home, "My *Father's* Home". When the true Church is complete and with her Head, and He can say, "Behold I and the children which God hath given Me" (Heb. 2 : 13), what perfect love and joy will pervade this Home, which will never be marred or broken up in any way for all within it will be as perfect as its Father. All who are to be at home with the Lord will be at rest in Him, and joy in Him (Isa. 67 : 2; Heb. 4 : 9; Matt. 25 : 21, 23). The felicity of this heavenly home will consist in free-dom from all evil, both of soul and body (Rev. 7 : 12); in the enjoyment of the Father as the chief good; in the com-pany of fellow-saints and the angels; in perfect holiness and extensive knowledge.

Heaven will also be a place where loving authority will be obeyed and eternally adored because of its awful majesty. This supernatural Heaven, with all its inner beauty, was partially seen by John who described this heavenly Jerusalem above as having foundations of sapphire, pinnacles of rubies, gates of carbuncles, borders of pleasant stones, with a beautiful river of clear, pure water flowing from the throne of the King around which is a gorgeous rainbow, similar to an emerald. After the Queen of Sheba had gazed upon the glory of Solomon, "there was no spirit in her". Before she came, she had heard of the fame and riches of Solomon, but after she had seen and heard all she had to confess "Behold, the half was not told me" (1 Kings 10: 1-9). Such will be our admiring confession when we see the King in all His beauty and behold the splendour of His palace. His wisdom and prosperity will exceed the fame we read and heard about here below.

Sufficient proof of Heaven as a place has been cited. As to its exact location, Scripture is silent. Death or the Coming of Christ to the air for His own will reveal the secret. Both the Bible and instinct point upward. Jesus was carried *up* to Heaven. Paul was caught *up* to the third heaven. Stephen in his martyrdom looked *up* into Heaven and saw Jesus standing to welcome him. John saw the Holy City coming *down*. All descriptions of Heaven in the Bible localize it as a place, as the final and eternal destination of the true believer. "Enoch was translated that he should not see death" (Heb. 11: 5). *Translate* means to transfer from one place to another. Enoch was not, for God took him. Where did God take His close companion to? Why, from earth to His own dwelling-place! Elijah was likewise transferred soul and body together to Heaven (2 Kings 2: 1, 11), and reappeared with Moses at our Lord's transfiguration (Matt. 17: 1-8).

Jesus prayed to His Father in Heaven where, before His Incarnation, He had lived from the past Eternity. There must be a place where the glorified body of the Saviour now is, for He ascended on high and there remains until "the times of restitution of all things" (Acts 3: 21). There he sits at the right hand of God in all His majesty (Heb. 1: 3); and where He is, there must also His servants be

(John 12: 26). The angels are spoken of as being in Heaven, and there must be a place where they assemble and from which they journey to and fro, carrying out Divine commissions on earth (Matt. 6: 10; 18: 10; Luke 2: 13–15; 22: 43; Ephes. 1: 10; Heb. 12: 22). In his dream, Jacob saw the angels ascending to and descending from Heaven. Varied answers have been given to the question, Where, and What is Heaven!

It has been variously described as "a state of happiness infinite in degree, and endless in duration", as "perfect purity, fulness of joy, everlasting freedom, health and fruition, complete security, substantial and eternal good".

Others assign to it "perfect rest, perfect love", "the day of which grace is the dawn, the rich ripe fruit of which grace is the lovely flower, the inner shrine of that most glorious temple to which grace forms the approach and outer court".

Another comment is "If one could look awhile through the chinks of Heaven's door and see the beauty and bliss of Paradise; if he could but lay his ear to Heaven and hear the ravishing music of those seraphic spirits and the anthems of praise which they sing, how would his soul be exhilarated and transported with joy."

While descriptions of Heaven in the Bible are not numerous there is one, prominent above others, we must ever bear in mind seeing it reveals the centre of attraction in Heaven, namely, the presence of the Lord Jesus Christ.

"Where Jesus is, 'tis Heaven there."

This we do know, that He is on the other side of the Glory-land waiting to welcome. It is His express wish that we should share Heaven with Him, "Where I am, there shall also My servant be" (John 12: 26). In His high-priestly prayer, He prayed, "Father, I will that they also, whom Thou hast given Me, be with Me where I am; that they may behold My glory" (John 17: 24). The disciples received the promise, "Where I am, there shall ye be also"

(John 14: 2, 3). All the saints are to be "for ever with the Lord" (1 Thess. 4: 17). To the dying thief who repented Jesus said, "Today shalt thou be with Me in Paradise". "Absent from the body" means "to be present with the Lord" (2 Cor. 5: 8). Paul wanted to depart this life and be "with Christ" which is far better (Phil. 1: 21–23).

> My knowledge of that life is small,
>   The eye of faith is dim;
> But 'tis enough that Christ knows all,
>   And I shall be with Him.

"Heaven is My throne," says God, and His beloved Son was ever near that seat of power and glory from the past Eternity. At His Incarnation, He surrendered the throne for a manger and then a Cross, but at His Ascension He returned to His natal realm—He went back home by His own merits and power to His rightful inheritance, and also as our Representative and Forerunner. Thus it is the Saviour who attracts our hearts and hopes to that blessed home where we are to be "For ever with the Lord. Amen! So let it be." In the Old Testament the emphasis was upon reunion with loved ones at death. Those who died are described as being "gathered unto their fathers". But in the fuller light of growing revelation, the saints are exhorted to think of death as the introduction to the Saviour—a gathering unto Him. "Gather My saints together unto Me; those that have made a covenant with Me by sacrifice" (Psalm 50: 5). Well might we exclaim, "Whom have I in Heaven but Thee? and there is none upon earth that I desire beside Thee" (Psalm 73: 25). Heaven, then, means that we shall see Him whom our souls love, and dwell with Him in the place He is presently preparing for us in His Father's Home.

The bliss of being with, and being like, Jesus will be the crown of happiness (Psalm 17: 15; John 12: 26; Rev. 22: 4). As it has been expressed:

The Light of Heaven will be the Face of Jesus;
The Music of Heaven will be the Name of Jesus;
The Theme of Heaven will be the Work of Jesus;
The Joy of Heaven will be the Presence of Jesus;
The Employment of Heaven will be the Service of Jesus;

We shall not be in Heaven for more than five minutes before we discover that—

> Christ is the heart of Heaven,
>   Its fulness and its bliss;
> The centre of the heavenly throng,
> The object of the ransomed's song,
>   Is Jesus in the midst.

John, the Apostle of Love, who had leaned on Jesus' bosom, lived so close to Heaven that a breath could have wafted him there. What a longing he had to see the Lamb in all His Glory in Immanuel's Land (Rev. 5: 6–14; 7: 9, 10, 17; 14: 1–3; 15: 3, 4). Had he known the lines of Horatius Bonar he would have sung them from his heart:

> When I shall gaze upon the Face of Him
> Who died for me, with eye no longer dim,
> And praise Him with the everlasting hymn,
>   I shall be satisfied.

How assuring and comforting are the following anonymous verses:

> He and I together entering
>   Those fair courts above.
> He and I together sharing,
>   All the Father's love.
>
>
> Where no shade nor stain can enter,
>   Nor the gold be dim,
> In that holiness unsullied
>   I shall walk with Him.

He and I in that bright glory
One deep joy shall share,
Mine, to be for ever with Him,
His, that I am there.

Are you not overawed as you contemplate what thrill will
be yours as you see Jesus for the first time and know Him
immediately by the print of the nails in His hand? We
have to confess that our sighings to be at home with Him
are not as intense as they should be. The Bible pictures
believers as groaning after Heaven. They lived *for*
Heaven, and longed to live *in* Heaven. May all of us
share the enthusiasm of that seraphic soul, Samuel Rutherford, who exclaimed:

> "Love Heaven. Let your heart be in it. Up, up and visit
> the new land and view the fair city, and the white throne of
> the Lamb—run fast for it is late."

We may be nearer Heaven than we expect. Glory may be
just round the corner. Who knows, the Saviour may be
about to say to your heart or mine, "Come up hither!" If
we are not to be ashamed before Him as we meet, our
lives must emit the fragrance of His inner presence as we
linger amid the shadows of earth. Our main business in
this world should be to secure an interest in the world to
come.

CHAPTER FIVE

The Occupations of the Occupants of Heaven

BECAUSE all of us are familiar with the Divine occupants of Heaven there is little need to linger over their identity. We know that *God* in all His unflecked holiness and majesty is there (Gen. 28: 16; Ps. 80: 14; Matt. 24: 36). Although, as we are told by John (1: 18) "No man hath seen God at any time, the Only Begotten Son, which is in the bosom of the Father, He hath declared Him". Our Father in Heaven is the Head of the sublime household. From all Eternity it has been His dwelling-place. The Lord God, Omnipotent and Almighty, waits to gather His children home. His finger is on the latch of the door, and because He is our loving heavenly Father we have the assurance of the homeliness of Heaven.

> God, my Father, waiteth there to greet me,
>   Child of His delight;
> In the well-beloved Son presented
>   Faultless in His sight.

Then *Christ*, God's only begotten Son, is there, and has been from the past Eternity. When He became Man, and lived among men for over thirty-three years, He was homesick for Heaven, and returned Home taking many with Him for He led captivity captive. He went back as the Redeemer and Intercessor of the saints and awaits the day when He can descend to the air to take the true Church to be with Himself (1 Thess. 4: 16).

The *Holy Spirit*, co-equal and co-existent with the Father and the Son, has shared the same glorious dwelling-place. Is He not the Eternal Spirit? These three, then, the great Trinity in Unity, are there in all their magnificent glory.

Along with the Father, Son, and Holy Spirit is the vast *Angelic Host* who add to the wonder and share in the glory of Heaven. Paul speaks of the celestial Intelligence as Archangels, Angels, Principalities, Powers, Thrones, Mights and Dominions (Rom. 8: 38; Ephes. 1: 20, 21; Col. 1: 16; Ps. 103: 19–21; Dan. 7: 10). Added to these are the unnamed beings "ten thousand times ten thousand, and thousands of thousands" (Isa. 6: 2; Heb. 12: 22; Rev. 4: 2; 5: 11). Our finite minds cannot comprehend what it means to dwell for ever with such an august assembly of holy beings who, with veiled faces, ascribe all honour and majesty to Him, sitting upon the throne.

The marvel of marvels is the presence in Heaven of the prophets, apostles, martyrs and saints of all ages, all dear to the heart of the Father because they were redeemed by the blood of His beloved Son and are not only "equal unto the angels" but are round about the throne as "sons of God, being sons of the resurrection" (Luke 20: 36; Rev. 18: 20). Their glorious inheritance was gained by Christ Who made them *joint-heirs*. An heir is one who inherits solely, by himself. A joint-heir is one who inherits with another. Thus, the property and riches of the Glory-land will be shared amongst all sinners saved by grace by the Lord Jesus Christ Himself. What a numberless throng of redeemed men, women and children all with celestial bodies will congregate together to live with God for ever! (Matt. 13: 43; Luke 20: 35, 36; 1 Cor. 15: 48.) In their glorified condition, with bodies changed and made like unto Christ's glorious body, "the God-consciousness will be supreme in them, holding both soul and body in absolute control, and shedding forth the full power of its glory without let or hindrance".

> On earth they sought the Saviour's grace,
>   On earth they loved His name;
> So now they see His blessed face,
>   And stand before the Lamb:
>   Singing Glory, glory, glory."

We now come to the fascinating aspect of the life and labours of the saints in Heaven. As glorified beings in a timeless world what knowledge, capabilities, progress and activities are theirs? How different will life be up there from what it is down here? Of this we are assured from the negative description or delineation of Heaven, that its bliss will largely consist in the absence of those experiences hindering our perpetual happiness on earth. Grouping seven negatives together we have:

No sickness, nor pain

Grateful, as we are, for doctors, hospitals and nurses who are at hand to help us as we endure the ills the flesh is heir to, it is blessed to know that in the New Jerusalem physical ailments and diseases can never attack the eternal life we are heirs of (Rev. 22: 2).

No hunger, nor thirst

Doubtless the majority of us have never experienced the pangs of hunger. In our affluent society we have an over-abundance. But around one in three in less privileged parts of the world live on the borderline of starvation. For the saints among them this promise of full sustenance must be comforting (Psalms 36: 8; 46: 4; Isa. 49: 10; Rev. 7: 16, 17; 22: 1, 2).

No sorrow, nor crying, nor tears

Daily, because of sin and separations, an ocean of tears are shed. The death of a friend He loved caused Jesus to weep. In the summer-land above no eyes are ever wet with tears for the causes of all tears are for ever removed (Isa. 25: 8; 35: 10; 51: 11; 65: 19). God's hand will be the handkerchief to wipe all our liquid grief away (Rev. 21: 4).

No sea

What separations the sea represents! Watch the heart-breaking farewells as loved ones leave by ship for another land. In Scriptures the sea is likewise the emblem of national unrest, turmoil and turbulence (Eccles. 1: 7; Isa. 57: 20; Jerm. 49: 23, margin Rev. 21: 1).

No death

As soon as a child is born it commences its pilgrimage to the grave. What with war, civil and otherwise, fearful road fatalities, ravaging diseases, and catastrophes in the realm of nature, Death is a busy reaper these days! But Heaven is a city without a cemetery. It is the deathless abode of Him Who is the Lord of Life (Hosea 13: 14; 1 Cor. 15: 26; Rev. 20: 14; 21: 4). The chill of a closed grave is never felt in Heaven.

No sin

We live in a world of sinners lost and ruined by the Fall. Sinners by birth, we become sinners by practice. "All have sinned, and come short of the glory of God," and sin is the sole primary cause of pain and privation, sickness and sorrow, disease and death (Gen. 3: 16–19; Eccles. 2: 22, 23; Rom. 5: 12; 8: 20–23). Describing Heaven, John says, "There shall be no more curse" (Rev. 22: 3). The world beyond will never be defiled by a single sin or sinner.

No night

The Bible uses *Night* to illustrate heathen ignorance
and profaneness—adversity—Death—danger, and robbers
who welcome the darkness for their crimes (Isa. 21: 12;
John 9: 6; Rom. 13: 12; 1 Thess. 5: 2). For those who
cannot sleep, night is a drag. Night can also represent
weariness. After a day of honest toil, how weary we are at
night. But there is no night in Heaven, and "no need of
light for the Lord God giveth them light" (Rev. 22: 5).
There is no need of sleep in Heaven.

> In that blest world above,
> Work never can bring weariness,
> For work itself is love.

Julia Sterling embodies these negatives in these expressive
lines:

> The Home beyond the shadows
> Hath neither pain nor tears;
> But, through its cloudless regions
> The Light of Life appears—
> Dispelling ev'ry sorrow,
> Removing ev'ry care,
> And giving rest eternal
> To all who enter there.
> Far away beyond the shadows
> Through gates that never close,
> There the King Himself will lead us
> Where the living water flows.

Turning to the positive descriptions of Heaven, we find
that they are necessarily largely figurative for human
language cannot depict heavenly glories in any other way
(Isa. 64: 4; 2 Cor. 12: 4, margin).

There will be pleasures for evermore

In the Divine Presence there is ever "the fulness of joy" which can enter our hearts even now (Pss. 16: 11; 21: 6, R.V.; 36: 8; Matt. 25: 21, 23). Many of our hymns are taken up with this aspect of Heaven. The lines of Ida G. Tremaine are assuring:

> A land of peace without alloy,
> Of joy beyond all earthly joy,
> And naught its calm can e'er destroy.

There will be rest from earth's weary labour

This does not mean a condition of inactivity throughout Eternity, as our next paragraph proves, but as Fanny J. Crosby puts it:

> After the weary conflict,
> Rest in the Saviour's love;
> After the pilgrim journey,
> Rest in the Home above.

There will be unceasing service

Further on, the reader will find a fuller section dealing with the occupations of the saved in Heaven. At present, we labour for the Master from the dawn to setting sun. After our earthly service ceases, and we reach Heaven, the nature of service will change (Rev. 7: 15; 22: 3). Even

> An angel's wing would droop if long at rest,
> And God Himself inactive were no longer blest.

There will be perfect knowledge

Because of our finite minds our knowledge of God and His ways is at best only partial. "Now we are looking in a mirror that gives only a dim, blurred reflection (of reality

64

as in a riddle or enigma), but then (when perfection comes) we shall see in reality and face to face" (1 Cor. 13: 9–12 *Amplified Bible*). With perfect understanding we shall experience that

> New discoveries are made
> Of God's unbounded wisdom, power and love,
> Which give the understanding larger room
> And swell the hymn with evergrowing praise.

There will be the perfection of safety and beauty

The great city, the holy Jerusalem, descending out of Heaven from God, had its walls and gates, suggesting *safety*, which were covered with gold and precious stones indicating *beauty* (Rev. 21: 1–21). What a combination this is for our adoring hearts to contemplate as Bernard of Cluny did when he wrote:

> True vision of true beauty
> True cure of the distrest,
> Beneath thy contemplation
> Sink heart and voice opprest;
> I know not, oh, I know not
> What joys await us there,
> What radiancy of glory,
> What bliss beyond compare.

There is a blissful reunion with loved ones who died in Christ

When Death bids us say *Farewell!* to those we love, it is comforting to know that the separation is only for a little. A blissful reunion awaits all who are the Lord's on yon heavenly shore. There are no "Good-byes" in Heaven (2 Sam. 12: 23; 1 Thess. 4: 13–18). With Dean Alford we can sing:

Oh then with raptured greetings,
On Canaan's happy shore,
What knitting severed friendship up,
Where partings are no more!
Then eyes with joy shall sparkle
That brimmed with tears of late;
Orphans no longer fatherless,
No widows desolate.

Coming to examine more definitely the life and lot of the redeemed in Heaven, there are many pertinent questions clamouring for an answer, which, if they cannot be answered from the Bible, either directly or by deduction, then silence should be observed. It is unwise to be dogmatic, speculative and imaginative where the Bible is silent. Among the many queries of the heart is, first of all:

The Question of Recognition in Heaven

A friend asked George Macdonald, the Scottish novelist and poet, "Shall we know one another in Heaven?" His pointed reply was: "Shall we be greater fools in Paradise than we are here?" Consciousness, fellowship, love, memory, personal identity, involve recognition. Each individual, *himself* or *herself* here, will possess hereafter a recognizable personality and faculties superior to those exercised on earth. We may not have the full understanding of the *mode* of recognition in Heaven but of the *fact* there need be no doubt. Paul reminds us that Heaven is the Home of "the whole family in heaven and earth" (Ephes. 3: 15). What kind of a Home would it be if its members are to be strangers to each other for ever? We can assume with certainty that we shall know one another more thoroughly in the life beyond. "Then shall I know even as also I am known" (1 Cor. 13: 13). Heaven means a more holy, blessed intimacy, our present human frailties prevent.

Further, this age-long and passionate desire has a strong sentimental value, and is likewise a perfectly legitimate one. Heaven would not be Heaven, if it does not offer reunion with, and the recognition of our dead in Christ. "All love is of God," John, the Apostle of Love, reminds us, and because love cannot be buried in a coffin, the beautiful but broken relationships of earth are resumed in the Father's home above where, as members of the same family we dwell together in perfect harmony.

The Bible offers sufficient evidence of recognition among the occupants of Heaven. We can be perfectly sure that the angels round about the throne of God know one another. Associated in the same service of praising the Lord, and carrying out Divine behests, we must infer that these glorious spirits know each other. Surely, the two angels found sitting at the Saviour's tomb, and who announced His Resurrection, recognized one another!

Further, the Old Testament saints believed that when they left earth they would join their relatives in another world and resume fellowship with them (Gen. 25: 8; 35: 29; 49: 33). Believing that Joseph was dead, Jacob said, "I shall go down into *sheol* unto my son mourning" (Gen. 37: 25). Actually, Jacob meant that he would go sorrowful into the other world there to be joined together again with Joseph. Jesus spoke about sitting down with Abraham, Isaac and Jacob in Heaven. How could we do this without recognizing them? What kind of a fellowship could they be if these patriarchs have not retained their identity? (Matt. 8: 11).

David, as he wept over his dead child, knew that he would join him again at death. "I shall go to him" (2 Sam. 12: 23). Remember, David had only seen the baby Bathsheba had borne him but a few days, yet he believed he would distinguish their baby from the millions in Heaven. David looked beyond the vast universe, to the place of reunion, saying, "My child is there. I shall go to him." The value of such a hope is better understood as we remember that David, as a man after God's own heart, knew as much about the mind of God, and the nature of the other world, as almost any other Old Testament writer. Did not King Saul recognize Samuel when God permitted him to return for a few brief seconds to announce Saul's doom.

Two men came down from the Glory-land to have a conversation with Jesus about His death at Jerusalem. Jesus had taken three of His disciples, Peter and James and John, to the summit of a mountain, and while there the two heavenly visitants appeared, Moses who lived 1350 B.C., and Elijah 870 B.C. (Matt. 17: 1–8). Peter, of course, had never seen these Old Testament saints in the flesh, yet he immediately recognized them for he said, "Let us make three tabernacles one for Moses, one for Elijah and one for Thee". Thus their identity must have been unimpaired.

The rich man in Hell recognized both Abraham and Lazarus (Luke 16: 19–31). While there is much of mystery in the incident Jesus related, this much is evident that there was unmistakable recognition. Identity had not been destroyed. Our Lord also taught that memory is immortal in the next world for Abraham said to Dives, "Son, remember that thou in thy lifetime receivedst thy good things". In His resurrection body, Jesus retained His identity. In the twilight Mary supposed Jesus to be the gardener. To all intents and appearance He was a human being, and as soon as He spoke Mary recognized the voice —the same voice that had previously spoken to her soul. The two disciples on the road to Emmaus did not recognize Jesus for the special reason Luke explains, "Their eyes were holden that they should not know Him". But later at supper, as He broke bread, the film fell from their eyes and they instantly recognized Him. "They knew Him" (Luke 24: 31). Paul would not have desired to be with Christ if he had not been sure of recognizing Him again as the One he saw on that road to Damascus (Acts 9; Phil. 1 : 21).

As to the righteous being able to converse with the Lord in Heaven, if we can speak to Him now in prayer surely we shall be able to do so more perfectly over there? How could we be "at home" with Him, and not recognize Him and be recognized by Him? Social fellowship, so far from ceasing in Heaven, will be vastly extended, and each of us will know intuitively the whole family of God. What a gathering of the ransomed that will be! If you have a dear one in Heaven your heart yearns to see, do not despair for you will meet again. The voice you loved to hear, you will hear again. The identity of the one you were near to on earth remains the same, and instant recognition will be yours as you meet never to part again. Your beloved one is only "lost awhile".

One of the great thrills in Heaven will be, not only that of meeting our dear ones again, but meeting the great saints of the ages, Abraham, Moses, David, Paul, and all the rest of the Prophets and Apostles as well as the martyrs and the worthies of the centuries, and as we meet them on the golden streets above, converse with them without restraint. As children of the same family, and all in Heaven through the grace of God introductions will be unnecessary as we shall all meet on the common ground of relationship. The poet asks:

> Shall we know the friends that greet us
> In that glorious spirit land?
> Shall we see the same eyes shining
> On us as in the days of yore?
> Shall we feel the dear arms turning
> Fondly, round us as before?

John Henry Newman, in *Lead, Kindly Light*, answers the question:

> And with the morn those angel faces smile
> Which I have loved long since and lost awhile.

The Question of Relationship in Heaven

Accepting the fact of recognition in the hereafter, the next question is: Are all the conventional relationships of this life to be continued in the life beyond? Do we carry over into the future state all the social associations of earth? The Sadducees sought an answer from Jesus about the relationship of the seven brothers married to the one woman, whom each man took as his wife, as each one died (Mark 12: 18–19). Surely she could not have the seven husbands around her in Heaven? Jesus answered that we shall be as the angels who, "neither marry nor are given in marriage" (Mark 12: 25). Our glorified bodies will be so changed that in our new environment, present bodily needs and desires will be extinct. As there is no propagation in Heaven, the new body will not have sexual organs; and as no material food will be required to sustain us, the new body will not have digestive organs. Hunger will not be ours for the Lord in the midst of the throne is to feed us. Animal and fleshy desires die with our animal nature. Spiritual affinities are to make us one in Heaven. All that is earthly and sensual in love is purged away. Ellicott comments, "The old relations may subsist under new conditions. Things that are incompatible here may there be found to co-exist. The saintly wife of two saintly husbands may love both with an angelic, and therefore a pure and unimpaired affection." But while sexual relations end with this life, we have no reason for believing that all social relations do also. True love is eternal, and the objects of this love on earth will be loved in a purer way above where life reaches a perfect fulfilment.

Heaven is not a sphere of ethereal, implied, cold, unsocial and formless spirits, but a Home of saints with glorified bodies having a perpetual interchange of perfect love and affection. Graven on the tombstone marking the place where Charles Kingsley and his much loved wife lie buried are the three Latin words, *Amavimus, Amamus,*

Amabimus, meaning, "We have loved, we love, we shall love." Such was Kingsley's faith, and such is ours. Over there we shall continue to love, only our love will be redeemed from all sensuality and grossness.

The Question of the Knowledge of our Departed

Enquiring hearts often want to know whether those in Heaven can see—whether they are cognizant of life here below—whether they know what is happening to us—whether they take an interest in our life and can pray for us. Expositors and commentators differ on such questions. The Bible nowhere clearly states that those in Heaven can see us at all times. If they could, they could hardly refrain from sorrow and tears as they view the troubles and sufferings of loved ones on earth. It may be that occasionally, by special dispensation, God allows those who have died to see those on earth, as in the case of the rich man and Lazarus, but aside from this account in Luke 16 there is little Scripture to support any contention that the dead have a continuing acquaintance with life on the earth.

A passage like that of being surrounded by "a cloud of witnesses" (Heb. 12: 1, 2) has been used to suggest that Heaven is not closed to earth, and that our warfare and welfare here below is still observed by those above; that our race is being run in an arena surrounded by those who have passed on before as spectators still interested in our spiritual progress. C. H. Spurgeon, in an eloquent sermon on this passage in which the writer speaks in the gymnastic style taken from the Olympic exercises:

"With a wave of the hand the Apostle directs us to the spectators who throng the sides of the course. There were always such at those races: each city and state fielded its contingent, and the assembled throng watched with eager eyes the efforts of those who strove for the mastery. Those who look down upon us from yonder heavens are described as 'so great a cloud of witnesses'. These compass us about.

Thousands upon thousands, who have run this race before, and have attained their crowns, behold us from their heavenly seats, and mark how we behave ourselves. This race is worth running, for the eyes of 'the nations of them which are saved' are fixed upon us. This is not a hole-in-the-corner business, this running for the great prize. Angels and principalities, powers and hosts redeemed by blood, have mustered to behold the glorious spectacle of men agonizing for holiness and putting forth their utmost strength to copy the Lord Jesus. Ye that are men, now run for it! If there be any spiritual life and gracious strength in you, put it forth today; for patriarchs and prophets, saints, martyrs, and the apostles look down from Heaven upon you."

We can imagine how those who listened to such descriptive preaching must have been carried away, but the fact remains that the narrative Spurgeon preached from *does not say* that those who have passed on are looking down on us from Heaven, but simply that we are surrounded by a company of witnesses namely, those heroes of faith mentioned in the previous chapter. Those worthies in Hebrews 11 lived lives testifying to the Faith. The word "witnesses" does not and cannot mean spectators. The Greek word for "witnesses" used here is *Martus* from which we have "martyr". These were men and women whose lives witnessed to the power of faith. Had the writer meant "spectators" he would have used *Autoptes* (Luke 1: 2) or *Epoptes* (2 Peter 1: 16).

The argument has been advanced that the departed can know about us without enduring pain because of trials here below. Our Lord does not suffer pain of heart, even although He looks down upon the sin and anguish of earth. He sees the end from the beginning, and with His vision of a glorious consummation does not sorrow as others. But Scripture, however, is silent on the question of Heaven being cognizant of earth, and our present welfare being the concern of dear ones above, it is best to follow the silence of Scripture and await the future. This fact is certain, that five minutes after death we shall have all the answers to our questions. At this point we can register our rejection of spiritualism or spiritism, which teaches that the dead do know all about us and can come back and converse with us through spiritualistic mediums. While there may be a good deal of quackery associated with séances, yet all is not false. So-called messages from the dead, if not the deliberate skilful manipulation and deception of mediums, may be the efforts of evil spirits who are able to impersonate the dead. The dead cannot return to commune with us, but as one writer suggests, "there is no reason why our Lord may not be properly asked, in submission of course to His will, to convey messages to our holy dead."*

Scripture, likewise, does not confirm the somewhat pleasing and sentimental assertion that our departed friends are silently and secretly with us, just as we have the spiritual presence of Christ; that loved ones are not separated from us in some far-off closed-up Heaven. John Oxenham, in a small poem of his, expresses the feelings of parents on learning that their son has died:

> He is gone . . . yet he is near us,
> Maybe he can see and hear us,
> Yes we feel him nearer, dearer,
> Tears have washed our souls' eyes clearer.

A similar sentiment of the nearness of our precious dead, can be found in these further lines:

> Linger a little, invisible host
> Of the saved dead, who stand
> Perhaps not far off, though men may scoff,
> Touch me with unfelt hands.

* *Note on Intercession of Departed Saints.* If our Lord is unceasingly active in intercession (Hebrews 7:25) and departed saints are said to be 'like Him', why should they not join Him in intercession? But see Revelation 6:9-11; 5:8-10. If we are to be priests, is not Intercession a priestly service?

The Question of Prayers for the Dead

Another problem concerning some bereaved hearts is whether those who have passed from their personal care and influence can be helped by constant intercession for them. Roman Catholicism teaches that there is a Purgatory where souls not bad enough for Hell and not holy enough for Heaven enter and that prayers, money and masses can help them out of Purgatory into Heaven. Martin Luther, the one-time Roman Catholic monk, said: "Since Scripture does not say anything about prayers for the dead, I do not concede it a sin if a man in his private devotions prays in terms like this: 'Dear Lord, if it is the case that this soul can be helped, then do Thou graciously etc.', and when this has been done once or twice let that suffice." J. Paterson Smyth in his volume *The Gospel of the Hereafter* relates this story which a friend told him: "I was a little child when the news came of my father's death, far away. That night, as usual, I prayed for him. But my aunt stopped me, 'Darling,' she said, 'you must not pray for Father now; it is wrong.' And I can remember still how I shrank back, feeling as if someone had slammed the door and shut Father outside." One of our poets has expressed a similar desire to surround the departed with our prayers in these lines:

How can I cease to pray for thee? Somewhere
    In God's wide universe thou art today.
Can He not reach thee with His tender care?
    Can He not hear me, when for thee I pray?
Somewhere thou livest and hast need of Him,
    Somewhere thy soul sees higher heights to climb,
And somewhere, too, there may be valleys dim
    Which thou must pass to reach the heights sublime.
Then all the more because thou canst not hear
    Poor human words of blessing, will I pray
O true, brave heart, God bless thee, whereso'er
    In God's wide universe thou art today.

But while Scripture has much to say about prayer and intercession, it gives no sanction whatever for prayers for the dead. Our eternal destiny is fixed before we pass over and no one and nothing can change that destiny. The person we die, whether saved or unsaved, that person we are on the other side for ever. For our dear ones who died in Christ all is well. They are with Him and safe in His care and keeping, and require no prayers of ours to help them. For those who died without Christ as their Saviour, prayers from this side cannot avail them. As Professor Wm. Clow puts it:

> "Beyond the fact that there is no record of prayer for the dead, there is the more conclusive fact that everywhere death is regarded as a change so decisive that the opportunities of life are closed finally and for ever . . . we cannot build a doctrine upon the feelings and desires of men. We cannot pray without knowledge, and any knowledge of the state of the dead is beyond our power."

But while Scripture says nothing about prayers for the dead, does it throw any light on the question of the dead praying for the living? There are a few references in *The Book of Revelation* to the prayers of saints who have gone on before, which may give us suggestions:

> "Golden vials full of odours, *which are the prayers of saints.*"
> "He should offer it *with the prayers of all saints* upon the golden altar which was before the throne. And the smoke of the incense which came *with the prayers of the saints.*"
> "I saw under the altar the souls of them that were slain . . . and *they cried,* 'How long, O Lord, holy and true, dost Thou not judge and avenge our blood on them that dwell on the earth' " (Rev. 5 : 6-8; 8 : 3, 4; 6 : 9, 10).

Believing, as we do, that the *Revelation* given to John was a Divine one, may it not give us food for thought that the passages above offer evidence that the saved departed can, and do, pray for us, even as Christ Himself in Heaven

prays for us (Rom. 8: 23; Heb. 7: 24, 25; 1 John 2: 1).
While on earth, those dear saints had us constantly in
their prayers, and although no longer here, they continue
such a gracious ministry on our behalf. And we owe more
than we realize to the prayers of these unseen saints whose
very intercession implies a degree of knowledge and
memory. We can only reverently leave the matter in the
hands of our Father.

The Question of Memory among the Dead

Closely allied to life, consciousness, and knowledge in
the after life is that of Memory. In Greek mythology,
Lethe represents the river of forgetfulness. It was supposed to be one of the rivers of Hades, which the souls of
all the dead are obliged to taste, that they may forget
everything said and done on the earth on which they had
previously lived. In the Greek, *letho* and *latheo* mean to
cause persons not to know. We have no Biblical evidence
that there is a river of such forgetfulness in Heaven. It is,
of course, blessed to realize that God has declared that He
will remember our sins and iniquities no more (Heb. 10:
17). When Solomon wrote, "There is no remembrance of
former things; neither shall there be any remembrance of
things that are to come with those that shall come after"
(Eccles. 1: 11), he was simply stating that those of one
generation are quickly forgotten by the succeeding generation but this statement has no relation to the heavenly
realm.

While Scripture does not say much about the immortality of memory, it does not leave us altogether without
light. There are passages clearly implying that Death does
not destroy our connection with the past; that our departed ones do not instantly forget those who loved and
cared for them while here below. The retention and quick-
ening of memory into fullest energy is surely evident in
the teachings of Christ and Paul:

"Every idle word that men shall speak, they shall give account thereof in the day of Judgment" (Matt. 12 : 26).

"So then every one of us shall give account of himself to God" (Rom. 14 : 12).

"We must all appear before the Judgment Seat of Christ, that every one may receive the things done in his body, according to that he hath done, whether it be good or bad" (2 Cor. 5 : 10).

The most convincing witness to the existence and function of memory in the next world is the incident our Lord related of Dives and Lazarus in the life beyond (Luke 16 : 29–31). Dives, the rich man, is in Hell not because he had been rich and fared sumptuously every day, but because he had neglected the higher, more character-forming influences of life. Lazarus was in a blissful Paradise not because he had been a poor beggar before his death, but because in spite of his extreme poverty and the leprous condition of his body—his "evil things"—he was rich in faith. When Dives prayed to Abraham to send Lazarus, no longer poor and diseased, to relieve his torment, and interceded not only for himself but his five brothers, Abraham replied:

"Son, *remember* that thou in thy lifetime receivedst thy good things, and likewise Lazarus evil things."

Alfred Tennyson has the couplet:

This is truth the poet sings,
That a sorrow's crown of sorrows is
remembering happier things.

The rich man's crown of sorrow was the remembrance of happier things; and, as Ellicott comments, the word *remember* our Lord used has "a terrible force in its bearing upon the question of the future life. Memory intensified, reproducing the past visions, pleasures and base joys, the *mala mentis gaudia* of the self-indulgent, and subject to the actions of a conscience no longer narcotised into slumber—this makes the sharpest pang of the deserved anguish." The call to recollection is clear and detailed, and witnesses to the fact that the departed can remember what happened here. Our blessed Lord Himself who, as the Great High Priest our nature wears, is not unmindful of His own on earth, and we have every right to think that our loved ones are not unmindful of us.

The question may arise, however, as to whether remembrance of much that happened here will not diminish the joy and dim the brightness of the glory of our departed. Doubtless this would be so, if it were not for the fact that our departed now see "the larger and ultimate purpose which events down here have served and are serving, and that makes all the difference". Because in Christ's immediate presence there is fulness of joy, those who are with Him cannot ever again be sad. Before the Cross, He said, "My soul is exceeding sorrowful", but now in glory, seeing and knowing all the sin, shame, suffering and sorrow of earth, His knowledge and memory do not make Him sad for He knows that He will yet see of the travail of His soul and be satisfied.

The sum of the matter then is that the faculties and powers which our dear ones possessed and exercised are not eliminated or cease to function when they passed from us. In the perfect world, every moral and spiritual quality is quickened and expanded. A part of George Klingle's moving poem reads:

> He does not mean—though Heaven be fair—
> To change the spirits entering there that they forget
> The eyes upraised and wet,
> The lips too still for prayer,
> The mute despair
> He will not take
> The spirit which He gave, and make
> The glorified so new
> That they are lost to me and you.

The Question of Progress in Heaven

It is because endless progress is man's unique destiny, that imperfect happiness is his peculiar lot here below. Our intellectual thirst for wide and deeper knowledge, and our spiritual aspirations for higher and noble moral achievements are "cribbed, cabined and confined" by the circumstances of our earthly existence. Browning wrote:

> Progress is man's distinctive mark alone—
> Not God's, and not the beast's; God, is, they are,
> Man partly is, and wholly hopes to be.

Wherever there is life there must be progress, and this applies to the life here and the life which is to come. In Heaven, we shall be continually growing, "not towards perfection, but *in* it". Many "gifts" are to pass away but faith, hope and love abide, because they are eternal (1 Cor. 13: 13). Faith is trust in God, and this will never end. Even in Heaven our hearts will cling to Him through whose grace we are in the realms of bliss. Here, faith often fails, but over there it will be always triumphant. Christian hope is expectation, and such expectation cannot die. In our heavenly progress new vistas of wonder will ever be opening up, new glories of our inheritance will ever be disclosed. Love for God, for the Saviour, for the Holy Spirit, for all the saints made perfect will become more pure and intense.

The knowledge we shall have in Heaven will be eternally potential and progressive? "Then shall I know even as also I have been known" (1 Cor. 13: 12). Our knowledge of God then is likened unto the knowledge He now has of us, and capacity then as now will be elastic. While it doth not yet appear what we shall be, we can expect to widen and deepen in maturity to all Eternity. Progressive knowledge here below is "hampered by many things; a perverted will, a beclouded mind, a divided heart, a fallible conscience, a dull vision, and by strictly limited

ability", says Dr. W. Graham Scroggie. But in our glorified body all will be different for then we shall have a will
in perfect accord with God's—a mind as clear as light—a
heart with only one passion that of love for God—a conscience knowing no wrong—our present faculties perfected, with the addition of others we have no conception
of. What a glorious prospect of expansion awaits the child
of God—a prospect inspiring us to rest content that "the
momentary lightness of tribulation works out for us an
eternal, excessively surpassing weight of glory" (2 Cor.
4: 17).

The Question of Degrees in Heaven

Although, through the grace of God every born-again
believer will be in Heaven, the further question arises as
to whether all the saints are to be on the same level there.
Are there to be degrees of position and glory in Heaven?
All God's people on earth are equal in His sight as far as
such a Divine relationship is concerned, but they are not
equal in respect to gifts, abilities, position and responsibilities.

How about Heaven? Are some of the saints to have
different and higher stations than others? There are those
who argue against any disparity, affirming that all the
people of God are loved by Him with the same love; were
all chosen together in Christ being equally redeemed by
His blood and equally interested in the same covenant of
grace and therefore are all on the same footing in respect
to service. To suppose the contrary, it is said, eclipses the
glory of Divine grace and carries with it the legal idea of
being rewarded for our work.

But Scripture expressly declares rewards in the hereafter for faithfulness in this world, and these rewards
contain nothing inconsistent with the Doctrines of Grace,
because those very works meriting reward were the effects
of God's own operation in and through His servants. By

graciously connecting degrees of blessing with obedience, God acts in harmony with His righteous character. Even His beloved Son has been highly exalted in Heaven for being obedient to the Divine will unto death. It is here that the Judgment Seat of Christ functions. "Every man's work is to be tried by fire," and the results of such a sifting will determine our place and position in our Lord's governmental control of all things. Thus, rewards are referred to as different *crowns*, and we must endeavour by the Spirit to "Hold that fast which thou hast, that no man take thy crown" (Rev. 3 : 11). A similar warning is given by John when he urges us to "Look to yourselves, *that ye lose not those things which ye have gained*, but that ye receive *a full reward*" (2 John 8). Many gain a reward. Others, a full reward. When Paul wrote of the possibility of becoming a *castaway* (1 Cor. 9 : 27), he was not referring to his soul but reward for service. The word "castaway" means "rejected" or "disapproved". *The Amplified Bible* translates the phrase, "I myself should become unfit—not stand the test and be unapproved—and rejected as a counterfeit". Paul was afraid lest after telling others how to live for Christ, he himself might at last fail so to do, and failing, forfeit the crown he had taught others to win.

We cannot emphasize too strongly that no truly born-again believer can lose his salvation for the simple reason that salvation is not *something* but SOMEONE. "Behold, *God* is my Salvation". Therefore how can a Christian possibly lose Him? Eternal life is a gift, and once received, becomes the possession of the recipient for ever. Recompense at the Judgment Seat of Christ will not come as a gift but a reward for the way in which we have served the Saviour. All the saints at that Judgment will inherit Heaven, but all within Heaven will not have the same capacity, position or responsibility. One is to have authority over "ten cities", and another over only "five", according to the use made of opportunity or responsibility here below (Luke 19 : 12–19). The many references to

Rewards emphasize the solemn fact that it matters very much how we live and labour here, seeing that the consequences of same are eternal.

In our Lord's teaching in the Parable of the Talents (Matt. 25), He makes it clear that where there is unequal ability but equal faithfulness the reward will be the same. In His Parable of the Pounds, He teaches that where there is equal ability but unequal faithfulness the reward will be graded. While consecrated living and serving bring a certain amount of reward now, the position in glory such merits will be determined at the Judgment Seat of Christ (Matt. 5: 12; 1 Cor. 3: 12–15; 2 Cor. 5: 10). To see a saint occupying a higher position than the one allotted to us will engender no jealousy or dissatisfaction. There will be no discontent among the saints in glory. *All* are to be satisfied when they awake with His likeness. This does not mean, however, that all are to have "the same capacity for enjoying God and Heaven, nor that all will have the same privilege of responsibility and authority, nor that all will have the same brightness of glory" (see 1 Cor. 15: 41). There would be no point at all in promised rewards for loyalty to Christ and His cause if at last all were to share alike. As Dr. J. D. Jones expresses it:

"There are differences in Heaven, differences of attainment and glory. There are some who are scarcely saved (1 Peter 4: 18; 1 Cor. 3: 15), and there are some who have an 'abundant entrance' into heavenly habitations (2 Peter 1: 11). And this fact of difference in attainment is quite compatible with the perfect blessedness of all. Each has all the blessedness he can contain. There is fulness of joy for all, though the capacity for joy may vary in each case."

The recurring promises and also solemn warnings should move us to daily watchfulness, to whole-hearted devotion to Christ, and to self-sacrificing service. Your work and mine is to be tried by fire of what *sort* it is (1 Cor. 3: 13)—*sort* not *size*. Commendation will be ours not for the *quantity* of our work but its *quality*. Only those who are *wise* are to shine as the brightness of the firmament and only those who *turn many to righteousness* are to shine as the stars for ever (Dan. 12 : 2). Only those who *suffer* with, and for Christ, are to *reign* with Him (2 Tim. 2 : 12). Only the *overcomers* are to receive the specified rewards (Rev. 2 : 7, 17, 26; 3 : 5, 12, 21). Only the *faithful* are to wear the specified *crowns* (1 Cor. 9 : 25; 1 Thess. 2 : 19, 20; 2 Tim. 4 : 7, 8; 1 Peter 5 : 4; Rev. 2 : 10). The tragedy is that many of us may face the Judgment Seat with a saved soul, but a lost life. There will be nothing to our credit. "Saved, yet so as by fire."

> In the strength of the Lord let me labour and pray
>   Let me watch as a winner of souls,
> That bright stars may be mine in the glorious day
>   When His praise like the sea-billows rolls.

The Question of the Service of the Glorified

We must get away from the traditional idea that the saints in Heaven have one eternal holiday; that they have nothing to occupy them save playing a harp and incessantly singing. Praise there will be, as we join in the Song of Moses and the Lamb, and likewise an eternal rest in Him. Leisure there will be, but a leisure in activity and service, as Frances Ridley Havergal expresses it:

Leisure to fathom the fathomless, leisure to seek and know
Marvels and secrets, and glories, Eternity alone can show;
Leisure of holiest gladness, leisure of Holiest love,
Leisure to drink from the Fountain of infinite peace
    above.

In Heaven, the Father, the Saviour, the Holy Spirit, and the Angelic Host are ever active. God controls the universe, and rules and overrules in the destiny of nations—the Saviour never ceases His advocacy and intercession on behalf of His own—the Holy Spirit is constantly occupied in convicting and regenerating sinners, and sanctifying the saints on earth—the Angelic Host serve God in multitudinous ways and minister on behalf of the heirs of salvation. When time is no more, and Christ delivers up the Kingdom to the Father, then many present aspects of the activities of the Trinity and the Angels in respect to earth and the saints thereon will cease. In the New Heavens and the New Earth, Divine industry will continue but in different ways, and the saints are to "serve Him day and night in His temple". All "His servants shall serve Him" (Rev. 22: 3). That the saints will be active we are plainly told, although the exact nature of service is not fully revealed. All will serve, but the extent and honour of service will be determined by the way we have lived and laboured here below (Matt. 25: 21; Luke 19: 17; 1 Cor. 6: 2; 2 Tim. 2: 12; Rev. 2: 27; 5: 10). Some of the faithful are to have authority over cities—others, rulers of many things—others, sitting on thrones and reigning (Matt. 25: 23; Luke 19: 17, 18; 22: 30; 1 Cor. 6: 2). The saints who are to reign must have subjects and these may consist of the nations saved. That renowned prophetic student Dr. Grattan Guinness said:

"As a king calls to his Cabinet his trusted and valued friends, and appoints to the most responsible posts those of the most approved fidelity, both for their reward and for the benefit of the kingdom, so with Christ and His saints. Those who have suffered are to reign with Him. We must not regard this as a figure of speech, but as the description of an actual reality."

Presently, the saints in glory may be occupied in intercession both for the saints and sinners on earth. If there is joy among the Angels over lost men and women repenting of their sin after being convicted by the Spirit of their need and peril, can we not visualize the triumphant above sharing in such angelic jubilation? As that interests God, interests the saints for they are one with Him.

Oh, for a nearer insight into Heaven,
　More knowledge of the glory, and the joy;
Which there unto the happy soul is given,
　Their intercourse, their worship, their employment.

It has been suggested that in Heaven we shall have opportunities of following our own particular bent to a perfection not possible on earth, and occupations so arranged as to exactly fit and satisfy each saint. Thinkers, painters and poets continuing their activity in a sunnier clime more conducive to the production of the best.

Each in his separate star
Painting the thing as he knows it
The Glory of Things as they are.

The late Sir Winston Churchill, among other things, was a first-rate artist although he was over forty years of age before he started to paint. He once wrote, "When I get to Heaven I mean to spend a considerable portion of my first million years in painting and so get to the bottom of the subject." Well, Churchill got far towards achieving that aim long before his death at ninety. But just what form of occupations are to be ours, the future alone will reveal. This we can be certain of, as Dr. Campbell Morgan has reminded us, that:

"Concerning the loved ones who have passed before us into closer fellowship with Christ, who have departed to be with Christ in a sense in which we never can be with Him here and now, am I not perfectly safe in supposing that the enterprise of His heart has become, in a measure never before possible, the enterprise of their hearts. . . . Those radiant flames of fire whose presence we so sadly miss; do not try to make me believe that they are doing nothing, resting merely, careless ever. Nay, nay; all that would imply the condition of Hell, not of Heaven. With Christ they feel His love; with Christ they co-operate in His service, and in closer union with God and Christ than ever realised here, they serve and work with Him always and ever towards the consummation upon which His heart is set, the infinite victory yet to come."

The Question of Heaven's Universal Language

The faculty of speech, and the words of the first language were divinely created and given. Man could never have invented a language. Adam is represented as immediately conversing with his Creator, using various words to express his thoughts. Whatever the Divine language was, Adam instinctively understood, and gave to the different animals names expressive of their habits and nature. What the primitive language was has been the matter of much dispute. It would seem as if it was *Hebrew*—the language God used in revealing His will to Moses and the prophets, and which was used until the Tower of Babel, a hundred years after the Flood, when God confounded *the* language of all the earth, that is, broke it up into other languages so that the people could not understand one another's speech (Gen. 10: 25; 11: 5–9). Now, there are hundreds upon hundreds of languages and dialects used all over the earth—and all because of sin and rebellion against God.

The present confusion, the babel of tongues and languages, make it difficult for us to converse with others of a different country. But in God's perfect Heaven there will be no rebellion. There, love and holiness and obedience will reign, and only one language, the language of Heaven, is spoken. One of the marvels of the Glory-land will be a perfect means of communication with one another and with God. There, tongues are to cease. Here below we have to employ an interpreter if we do not know the language of a foreign country which we may be visiting. Think of the years it takes a missionary to learn the language and various dialects of tribes he has dedicated his life to Christ to evangelize. As saints from India, Africa, Japan, China, English speaking countries, and

European countries enter Heaven, what strangers they would remain if they took with them their own native tongue. But as Heaven represents perfect fellowship among its inhabitants, they must be able to converse freely and understandably with one another. Then, the people of God will be one, having one language, as the human race had at the beginning. There will be no need up in Heaven for the Lord to speak so that every man may hear in his own language, as at Pentecost (Acts 2: 6). Throughout His courts above, Saints and Angels will converse in Heaven's own tongue, and together magnify the Lamb with one heart and voice and language. How overwhelming the prospect!

The Question of Little Children in Heaven

No more brutal and false doctrine was ever concocted than that which asserts that unbaptized children go to perdition. Such monstrous teaching is absolutely contrary to the character of God, and opposed to the evangel of Christ. Even Augustine could actually bring himself to teach that all children dying unbaptized in the Roman Church would be damned! Something of this blasphemous and ghastly teaching can be found in a volume for children by a Roman Catholic priest, the Rev. Father Furniss, bearing the title, *The Light of Hell*. This book contains matter which is positively too horrible even to quote. All that we can say is that any man who could write such terrible and senseless words was of the devil himself. How destitute of compassion he must have been, and how different his attitude from that of the Master who said of the children, "Of such is the kingdom of Heaven". Bless God, there are no babies and children under the age of responsibility in Hell!

Dying before they reached the years of moral choice and the power to discern between right and wrong, they passed right into the presence of Jesus in virtue of His atoning work upon the Cross. Original sin they did have, but that was covered by the Blood. Practised sin they did not have and therefore were not guilty of transgressions incurring the wrath of God. As for the mentally deficient, if born insane, they enter Heaven upon the same conditions.

> How came those children there,
> Singing Glory, Glory, Glory?
>
> Because the Saviour shed his blood
> To wash away their sin,
> Bathed in that precious purple flood,
> Behold them white and clean,
> Singing, Glory, Glory Glory.

A matter perplexing the heart of many a Christian mother who has a baby in Heaven is whether that little one will remain in the same state above. Do girls and boys have their purpose in Heaven as such? A twin answer is offered for this question. First, there are those who feel that without children in Heaven much would be missed by the godly parents who bore them; that as we depart whether child, youth or patriarch, so we remain; that when the body is raised at Christ's Return, He will raise it as it was but withal glorified. Thus, a child of one year will still be, in size and appearance, a child a year old; that a mother will have her child as a *child* for ever. Preaching on the theme of Recognition in Heaven, Bishop Simpson of America broke out in his sermon with the question, "What would Heaven be to me without my Willie?"— Willie being his dear son whom death had recently claimed.

The second approach is that growth and increase will be characteristic of children in Heaven; that the mother crossing the threshold of the life beyond will instantly discover that her child, or children, have grown to a glorified maturity. Under the creative touch of God, and under the tutelage of their angel-teachers they steadily grew into a perfect character. F. C. Spurr tells of a friend of his who had lost a child, and who sent him a silver printed card bearing the words:

"In memory of our little Donald,
lent to us for two years; the sunshine of our home,
recalled by the Father,
now at school with the angels for his tutors."

Such a hope is a comforting and satisfying one for those who believe that the lambs gathered to His bosom reach the full stature of glorified manhood or womanhood. Just what the exact future holds for the children who die before their innocency is blasted by the sins of this life, Scripture does not say. In this faith, however, we can rest that our dear ones are not lost to us, and that no matter what change may overtake them, they will still be ours; and that all the redeemed, like the angels, will possess endless youth, activity, power, knowledge and holiness; and experience the same immortal happiness, dignity and Divine favour; be lovely, beautiful and glorious in the sight of God.

My knowledge of that life is small,
    The eye of faith is dim;
But 'tis enough that Christ knows all,
    And I shall be with Him.

An error that must be corrected is that children, or for that matter, all the saints, are to be angels in Heaven. That hymns are not always Biblical is evident from the children's one, a verse of which reads:

I want to be an angel
    And with the angels stand;
A crown upon my forehead,
    And harp within my hand.

Our Lord clearly taught that we are to resemble the holy angels in some of their attributes, but never that we are to be angels. All the saints in Heaven will be glorified human beings, as distinct from the angels, as they are distinct from the Lord of Glory. Neither are we to spend Eternity "singing around the throne" with harp in hand. Song there will be, but also Service, fitted to our individuality. As real beings, possessed of spiritual bodies and quickened intellects we shall be active, serving the Lord as we cannot here below because of the trammelling influences of the flesh.

On earth the broken arcs, in Heaven the perfect round.

It is true that we are to rest from our labours, but the word for *labour* here means "a painful strain"—a feeling never experienced in Heaven where eternal, untiring youth and strength will be ours in the carrying out of God's glorious commissions. In His Temple there will be no long sermons and meaningless ritual, but a delightsome and unceasing serving and rejoicing. Weariness and tedium will never be ours. Only a constant, happy, and privileged activity. As Dr. Alexander Smellie so beautifully expresses it:

"God bring me to Jerusalem! God bring me home in peace! It is the heart's uttermost attained at length. It is the heart's harbour made after the stormy sea.

"There my senses will be marvellously transfigured and sublimed; so that I shall hunger no more and thirst no more, and I shall behold Christ's face, and I shall hear the songs of the seraphim.

"There my intellect will have its doubt resolved and its mysteries cleared, and I shall know even as also I am known.

"There my memory will cease to be haunted by grievous recollections of past sins; for I shall live in the presence of my Saviour, and His grace will be all my thought.

"There my conscience will have its alarms stilled and its perplexities made plain; it will see and follow Him Who has brought in for it a perfect righteousness.

"There my will will never be visited by uprisings of

rebellion and disobedience; Jesus will lead me in perpetual triumph behind His chariot-wheels.

"There my affections will be satisfied. 'I go,' as Jacob Böhme said, 'to be with my Redeemer and my King in Paradise.'

"O, sweet and blessed country!"

Wise theologians of old divided the happiness of Heaven into what they called the *Essential* and *Accidental* joys. By *Essential* they implied the satisfaction the soul derives immediately from God's Presence, and from the beatific vision.

> What rapture will it be
> Prostrate before Thy Throne to lie,
> And gaze and gaze on Thee.

The great and crowning truth about the heavenly life awaiting us is that it will be a life eternally lived in un-speakable glory. The disciples had a fleeting glimpse of that glory when, on the Mount of Transfiguration, they were eye-witnesses of the Lord's majesty. Ours will be the privilege of basking continually in the full blaze of that glory. Samuel Rutherford, that seraphic, covenanting preacher, fell into raptures whenever he thought of Heaven:

"Oh, how sweet and glorious shall our case be when that Fairest among the sons of men will lay His fair face to our sinful eyes and wipe away all tears from our eyes. O time, run swiftly, and hasten that day."

Similarly, we find Augustine expressing the same hope:

"Christ shall be the end of all our longing and desire! Him shall we perpetually see! Him shall we love without tediousness and grief! and Him shall we praise without ending."

> Just to be near the dear Lord I adore,
> That will be glory—be glory for me.

By *Accidental*, the old divines implied those additional joys coming from reunion with loved ones and friends; meeting the saints of all ages; joyous occupations, all the delights of ever-widening knowledge. A multitude of secondary joys will spring from the many surprises Heaven holds for us—Christians will be there we hoped to meet; and some will be there we had no thought of seeing. The marvel of marvels is that through infinite grace we shall be there ourselves.

> I stand upon His merit;
>   I know no other stand,
> Not even where glory dwelleth
>   In Immanuel's land.

CHAPTER SIX

The Significance of Abraham's Bosom
and Paradise

Paradise is a beautiful term of Persian origin, and meaningful as it is musical. Its original significance was that of "a foreign ornamental garden" attached to a palace or mansion. The word is translated as a "garden" or "orchard" (Neh. 2: 8; Eccles. 4: 13; S. of Sol. 4: 13), and is used of Adamic Eden (Gen. 2: 18; 3: 23; Joel 2: 3), the habitation of man in his state of innocence, in which he enjoyed that presence of his Creator, which constituted his supreme happiness. The Bible teaches, however, that man must have no Paradise on earth, but seek one to come, even "a better country". No matter how lovely an earthly paradise may be man's, it can never make up for the loss of a heavenly Paradise (Rev. 2: 7; 22: 1, 2, 14). In the Talmudic tradition Paradise is not Eden, but rather a heavenly place—a park-garden of God—of somewhat indistinct dimensions, suitable for mystic enquiry, with rooms and dwellings, commensurate with the record of men. The Valley of Jordan became "the paradise of God" (Gen. 13: 10).

In the New Testament, Paradise represents the invisible residence of the blessed. It is the term given to the blessed resting place with Jesus to which the penitent went until the resurrection (Luke 23: 43). The Jews identified Paradise as the Heaven into which Enoch was translated. Paul was caught up to the third heaven, identified as Heaven (2 Cor. 12: 24). Because the word *Paradise* was used to describe gardens of unparalleled beauty and splendour, we can readily understand why the word is used to illustrate the realms of spiritual bliss. Scripture is silent on its exact location and nature. The question arises as to the immediate abode of the soul at death. In his *112th Sermon*, we find John Wesley affirming that, "It is plain that paradise is not Heaven. It is, indeed, if we may be allowed the expression, 'the ante-chamber of'." Origen, the early Father reckoned somewhat heterodox by the other Fathers, plainly stated, "Not even the Apostles have received their perfect bliss, for the saints at their departure out of this life do not attain the full reward of their labours, but are awaiting us, who still remain on earth, loitering though we be and slack."

Does man exist in three states as some teach who believe in an intermediate, or waiting period? Namely:

> On earth with body and soul united.
> After death with the body in the grave and the soul in Hades.
> After the resurrection with the body and soul united, in the final abode.

The Jews taught that there are four divisions in Sheol:

> One for those who were martyred for righteousness sake;
> One for sinners who on earth had paid the penalty for their sins;
> One for the just who had not suffered martyrdom;
> One for sinners who had not been punished on earth.

Among Alexandrian Jews the view prevailed that the separation of the righteous from the wicked took place immediately after death which seems to be the underlying idea in the New Testament use of the word *Paradise*. What, exactly, is the position in this matter? Where does the spirit go, and what becomes of the dispossessed inhabitant of "the earthly tabernacle"? We, herewith, set forth what we deem to be the most satisfactory explanation of any pre-resurrection state.

Up until the Ascension of our blessed Lord, the departing did not go direct to their final abode in Heaven or Hell, but to an intermediate state of disembodied spirits in an abode having two divisions or compartments. *Hades* or its corresponding word *Sheol* represents the state and abode of the dead in general.

1. *Before the Ascension* we find:
One part, called *Hell, The Pit, Tartarus* (Rev. 9: 1, 2, 11; 2 Peter 2: 4, R.V.) where the wicked and all Christ-rejectors are found (Luke 16: 23).

The other part was known as *Paradise*, or Abraham's Bosom, the place where the righteous or the saved were found (Luke 16: 23; 23: 43). From our Lord's teaching at this point, it is clear that death is not an end but the beginning of an eternal existence, that in the unseen world the departed are alive, conscious, and in the full exercises of their faculties such as memory, the ability to feel pain as in the torment of the rich man, as well as in his concern over his five brothers who were on the way to the same place of anguish.

The writer of "The Book of Enoch" declares that "Raphael, one of the holy angels," showed him "hollow places, deep and very smooth, and three of them were dark and one bright"; explaining that "these hollow places have been created for this very purpose, that the spirits of the souls of the dead should assemble therein . . . till the great judgment comes upon them. . . . This division has been made for the spirits of the righteous . . . and this has been made for sinners."

In "the great gulf fixed", our Lord declared the impossibility of contact between the saved and the lost—which final exclusion cuts out any thought of Purgatory from which ultimately the condemned can be transferred to Heaven. In spite of the claims of the Roman Catholic Church, the Bible knows nothing of such a Purgatory between the abode of the lost and Heaven. As Professor Wm. Clow expresses it:

> "When Jesus, in the narrative of the rich man and Lazarus says, 'The rich man also died, and was buried, and in Hell he lift up his eyes,' as though these were three instantly succeeding events, He seems to bar the mind after any theory of after-salvation. The great saying, 'Today shalt thou be with Me in Paradise', and His own simple statement: 'I go to My Father' all imply that for Jesus the soul passed at death either into the presence of God or into that limbus where God's mercy was not proclaimed."

In verse J. J. Sims combines the same finality thus:

> The tide is flowing out,
> We're drifting to the sea;
> Drifting out to darkness, far from love and light
> Where the storms are raging, into endless night;
> Or drifting on to glory, past all pain and care,
> Into Heaven's brightness, where the ransomed are.

2. *After Christ's Ascension* a change took place in the long abode of departed spirits.

One division or compartment was emptied. Christ's death upon the Cross was not like the extinguishing of a candle. Dying in anguish and shame, He comforted His repentant companion in suffering with the assuring words, "Today shalt thou be with Me in Paradise" (Luke 23: 43). And, as Dr. G. F. Wright reminds us in his article on *Paradise*:

> "The consolation needed by the penitent thief suffering from thirst and agony and shame was such as was symbolized by the popular conception of Paradise, which, as held by the Essenes, consisted of 'habitations beyond the ocean, in a region that is neither oppressed with storm of rain, or snow, or with intense heat, but that this place is such as is refreshed by the gentle breathing of a west wind, that is perpetually blowing from the Ocean."

The moment Christ and the believing thief died they went to the section described by Christ as "Abraham's Bosom". Recognizing Christ as a true King, the thief prayed that he might be remembered by Him when He came into His Kingdom. "Abraham's Bosom" was not His Kingdom, although all the saints within it owned Him as Lord. When He returns to earth as its rightful Lord and King it will be to inaugurate His Kingdom. During the three days and three nights His Body reposed in Joseph's new tomb, the Crucified One Himself was in the division where the holy ones were as happy "prisoners of hope". We can imagine how Jesus preached to these righteous spirits in the ante-chamber of Heaven, about their immediate ascension to Heaven itself.

After His Resurrection our Lord spent forty days among His own, during which period He fully instructed them as to their witness in the world, and the message they should unashamedly proclaim by the power of the Holy Spirit (Acts 1: 1–5). After commissioning the disciples, the further miracle happened and Jesus ascended on high—taken up from them into Heaven (Acts 1: 8–11). Dwelling upon His return to the Father's Home, Paul says that, "When He ascended up on high He led a multitude of captives" which is the marginal reading for the phrase, "He led captivity captive" (Ephes. 4: 8–11). Who were those represented by this "body of captives"? One interpretation is that by His Death and Resurrection, Christ triumphed over "principalities and powers" (Col. 2: 15), that is, the powers of sin and death, making a show of them openly, triumphing over them in the Cross.

We do not feel, however, that this explanation fully exhausts the significance of the apostolic phrase of Christ leading "captivity captive" when He ascended on high. Paul reminds us that before His Ascension on high, Christ descended first into the lowest parts of the earth, or into the realms below. It is true that at His Incarnation, He descended from Heaven to earth, and that in His Death,

His body went still farther into the earth. But is this the limit of interpretation regarding His descent into the earth? The Hebrew idea was that *Sheol*, or the abode of all departed spirits, was in the bowels of the earth. It would seem, therefore, that what transpired was after this order. When Christ ascended, He marshalled all the saints in "Abraham's Bosom" together and as the Conqueror, having the keys of Death and Hades, He took them to Heaven with Him into God's immediate presence. As Heaven is the goal of all who are the Lord's now, in this age of grace, when a believer dies he or she goes to Heaven. "Absent from the body, present, or, at home, with the Lord." No longer are the saints gathered into "Abraham's Bosom" or into "Paradise", but unto Christ. If we die *in* Him, we go to be *with* Him. And where is He? At the Father's right hand of the majesty on high (Heb. 1 : 3).

With the one section of *Sheol* empty—the Paradise division—what about the part Christ depicted as being associated with torment? There has been no change of place or condition revealed in Scripture for those who die out of the Lord. The *Hell* He spoke of is now stiffened into its more terrible meaning. Such a Hell, with all its remorse and anguish, is not the final abode of the wicked, just as the other section, namely, "Abraham's Bosom" was not the final resting place of the righteous. At the Judgment of the Great White Throne, all the wicked dead are to be raised for the ratification of their condemnation. "Death and Hell delivered up the dead which were in them. . . . Whosoever was not found written in the book of life was cast into the Lake of Fire", the latter being the final and eternal depository, not only of the wicked but also of Satan, the Beast, the False Prophet, Death and Hell (Matt. 25: 41; Rev. 20: 10–15; 21: 6 see 2 Peter 2: 6; Jude 6). How solemn is the truth that nothing but the blackness of darkness for ever awaits all those who die in their sins! The rich man's concern, while in Hell, over

98

his five brothers, whom he knew to be travelling to the same place of doom, was unavailing. It was too late for him to warn them to flee from the wrath to come. Still on this side of Eternity with ample opportunity to "rescue the perishing and care for the dying", are we moved with Calvary's passion and compassion for the lost? Will there be fewer sinners in Hell because of our undying desire to win souls for Him who died that they might not perish? "*Now*—only now in this Gospel age—is the Day of Salvation." Death seals our destiny to glory or despair.

O God, to think the countless souls that pass away
　Through each short moment that we live,
Destined to dwell in Heaven or groan in Hell for aye.
　O stir me up, and new strength give,
And let not one pass out through death in shame and sin,
That I through Thee might seek and win.

Returning to the fact already expressed, namely, that there is no intermediate or interim state for the believer, no ante-chamber for him to reside in until the resurrection at Christ's Return (1 Thess. 4: 13–18), we take cognizance of those who have thought and taught that there is a temporary place of blessedness for the saints before going to the ultimate home of the redeemed. Some of the early Christian Fathers held the view of the immediate, but not perfect, bliss of the saved. Tertullian, writing at the end of the second century, said:

"The souls of all men go to Hades until the Resurrection, those of the just being in that part of Hades called 'the bosom of Abraham' or 'Paradise'."

Augustine, at the end of the fourth century, put it thus:

"The time between Death and the final Resurrection holds the soul in hidden receptacle, according as each soul is meet for rest or punishment."

The phrase "under the altar" (Rev. 6: 9–11; 16: 9) is made for signifying complete security, but suspended perfection. Our contention, however, is that as Christ has been in Heaven since His Resurrection, and assured us that where He is there shall we be also, that when a child of His dies he or she goes immediately to be with Him in the Father's home above. Does not Paul affirm that when Jesus leaves Heaven for the rapture of the saints, He will bring *all* the saints who are presently in His presence *with* Him? (1 Thess. 4: 14).

As yet, those who died in the Lord do not have the glorified, eternal body, and will not, therefore, be completely like Him in this respect until He comes the second time (1 John 3: 1–3). What kind of a covering do they have? Paul, yearning for his glorified body, did not want to be found "unclothed" or "naked" (2 Cor. 5: 1–4). As the Scripture is silent on the exact nature of a temporary covering, it is but fitting to emulate its silence. This we do know that when Jesus went to Paradise along with the dying thief, His natural body remained in Joseph's tomb, and that on the Sabbath morning His spirit re-entered it and it became the deathless body He ascended to Heaven with. What covering He had for His spirit during His period in Paradise awaiting His Resurrection we are not told. God speaks of Himself as clothing Himself with honour and majesty, and clothing Himself with light as with a garment (Ps. 104: 1, 2). Who knows, perhaps He has a similar provision for us until we reach what Paul calls "the redemption of the body" (Rom. 8: 23). Presently, the new life within is encased in a mortal, corruptible body. But, says Paul, "we shall all be changed", and such a glorious transformation will be ours when Jesus comes and we shall be raised with a perfect, incorruptible body like unto His. What a day that will be when:

> On the Resurrection Morning
> Soul and body meet again;
> No more sorrow, no more weeping,
>   No more pain!

CHAPTER SEVEN

The Only Persons Heaven Receives

As our minds become imbued with false ideas about Heaven and those eligible to enter the "realm of eternal bliss", it is as well to consult the only infallible guide to Heaven in order to discover how to get there, and who are welcomed over its borders. Not all are admitted who feel they have every right of entrance. Lord Byron wrote of those who, "In hope to merit Heaven by making earth Hell". But nothing a person may be able to do can possibly merit him Heaven. A Christ-rejector, debauched and licentious deserves Hell, and will endure it if he dies in his sin and unrepentant. The best person in all the world, however, with all his good and noble deeds, is undeserving of Heaven, for presence therein is all of Grace. A consecrated Christian, faithful in all his stewardship, qualifies for coming responsibilities *in* Heaven, but his prospect of going *to* Heaven is bound up with the merits of Christ. It is because of the acceptance by faith of all that He accomplished on our behalf that Heaven becomes ours. Heaven cannot be earned; it is the final instalment of the gift of Salvation. "The Lord will *give* grace, and glory." We stand now in Grace because of it, and ultimately shall receive Glory. It has been truly said that a man may go to Heaven

Without health,
   Without wealth,
      Without fame,
         Without a great name,
            Without learning,

> Without big earning,
> Without culture,
> Without beauty,
> Without friends,

Without 10,000 other things.

> But he can
> Never go to Heaven
> Without Christ.

Robert Browning has the couplet:

> Lose who may—I still can say
> Those who win Heaven, blest are they.

While we understand the sentiment of this renowned poet, correction is necessary about the idea of Heaven being *won*. Paul certainly wrote about winning the race, winning Christ (Phil. 3: 9), but his exhortation has nothing to do with trying to win a place in Heaven by our own energy, sacrifice, and efforts. By winning, or *gaining* Christ, as the word means, implies finding Him and laying hold of Him by faith which does not depend upon the sole action of the individual as Paul goes on to add "that I may . . . be found of God in Him", that is, drawn into union with Christ by the grace of God, so that we may "dwell in Him, and He in us". By the might of the Holy Spirit we can run the race, having our eyes on the prize, which is a reward in Heaven. But Heaven itself cannot be won by human endeavour. It is the gift of God.

There are other unscriptural ideas of Heaven we must rid the mind of such as, Peter having the keys of Heaven, with power to admit or reject any who approach its gates. The right to enter the Father's House above depends upon our relationship to His beloved Son, the Saviour of the World and not upon any capriciousness of Peter. Only those who "die in the Lord" go to be "with the Lord"; and if we are to die in the Lord we must live in the Lord as we linger here below. Further, it must be emphasized that the beginning of Heaven is not at that hour when the eye grows dim, and the sound of friendly voices becomes silent in death, but at that hour when God draws near and the eyes of the spiritual understanding are opened, and the soul sees how hateful sin is in the sight of a thrice-holy God, and how all-sufficient and wonderful Christ is as the Saviour. The hour when self-will is crucified and the God-will is born in the resolution of a new heart is the hour Heaven begins.

There are those who affirm that no matter how degraded a sinner may be within him is "the Divine spark", which waits to be found and fanned into a glowing flame. But the Bible says that in us, that is in our flesh, dwelleth *no good thing*. Regeneration is not the development of any innate feeling after God but the impartation of the Divine nature. When Jesus said, "The Kingdom of God is within you", He did not mean to imply that Heaven is *something* within us rather than a place *somewhere* outside of us—a state rather than a sphere—character rather than a country. His statement can be translated, "The Kingdom of God is among you", as it actually was in Himself for in all His ways and works He was the Personification of the Kingdom.

We disagree with those who affirm that Heaven or Hell are conditions of inward character and not merely places to which we are sent arbitrarily. We believe Heaven to be a place of residence and not a state of character, although all who are on their way to Heaven should live in the heavenlies in Christ Jesus, and therefore emit the fragrance of the heavenly abode. While our position in Heaven depends upon our faithfulness to Christ and His cause (Rev. 2: 10), Heaven itself comes to us in consequence of accepting the Lord Jesus Christ as a personal Saviour. We readily grant that some men live hellish lives, while others are heavenly, but Heaven and Hell as definite spheres, and not merely a state of mind commenced on earth and developed beyond it. In speaking of the Father's Home, and of His preparation of a place therein for all those who are His, Jesus said:

"I am the Way, the Truth and the Life, no man cometh unto the Father but by Me" (John 14 : 6).

Thus, with Heaven in mind He said, "I am the Way" there; and no man, no matter who he is, or what he has done, can enter except through My mediation." *But by Me!* Let us not lose sight of this authoritative statement for whether we think of *Salvation*, or *Worship*, or *Heaven*, we have no access whatever to God apart from all His beloved Son accomplished on our behalf. If our feet are not on *The Way* to Heaven, then how can we expect to reach and enter it? Therefore, any heart in which Christ is not enshrined as Saviour and Lord is destitute of any hope of Heaven.

Archbishop Ramsey, head of the Anglican Church, tells us that "Heaven is also not a place to which humans go in our present bodily state, nor is it a place for Christians *only*. Those who have led a good life on earth, but found themselves unable to believe in God, will not be debarred from Heaven. I expect to meet some present-day atheists there." But such a pontifical pronouncement is entirely alien to the teaching of Christ, and to the Bible as a whole. Any minister speaking in this way is a blind leader of the blind. Jesus declared that it is *only* those who believe in Him who have everlasting life (John 6: 47); and that it is *only* those who confess Him before men that He will confess before His Father in Heaven (Matt. 10: 32). The Bible gives us a long list of those who will never enter Heaven. Here is Paul's catalogue:

"Now the works of the flesh are manifest which are these: adultery, fornication, uncleanness, lasciviousness, idolatry, witchcraft, hatred, emulations, wrath, strife, seditions, here-sies, envyings, murders, drunkenness, revellings and such like: of the which I tell you before, as I have also told you in times past, that they which do such things *shall not* inherit the kingdom of God" (Gal. 5 : 19–21).

That Heaven will not admit anything nor anyone alien to the holy character of God is clear from *The Revelation* given to John, the Apostle of Love:

"There shall in no wise enter into Heaven anything that defileth, neither whatsoever worketh an abomination, or maketh a lie: but they which are written in the Lamb's book of life" (Rev. 21 : 27, see 21 : 8; 22 : 18, 19).

Maketh a lie! Archbishop Ramsey says he hopes to see *atheists* in Heaven. Who is an atheist but one who makes a liar of God, whose existence is not only proclaimed in Scripture, but in the marvellous universe He created. The misguided Archbishop fails to realize that if there is no God, as the atheist asserts, then there can be no Heaven, spoken of as His Home. Further, if atheists can go to Heaven, then there is no need of the Church, or of the Gospel it should preach whereby men are warned of their eternal doom if they die out of Christ. The Apostle affirms that impurities and sinners of all kinds and degrees are excluded from Heaven, and that *only* those who are registered on the grand roll of Redemption are admitted. Somehow, we prefer to believe the Spirit-inspired Apostle, rather than a benevolent yet unbiblical Archbishop.

In his illuminating study on *Immortality* Professor James Denny has this to say regarding the necessity of faith in Christ if Heaven is to be entered:

"Faith in immortality, which is moral and spiritual through and through, rests upon a supreme revelation of what God has done for man and *involves present life in fellowship with the Risen Savious,* and is neither worldly nor other-worldly, but Eternal, and has propagated itself *fellowship with the Risen Saviour,* and is neither worldly governing faith of *believing men and women in proportion as they realise their union with the Saviour*—a faith infinite

in its power to console and inspire. . . . Faith in immortality
has in point of fact entered the world and affected human
life along the line of *faith in God and in Jesus Christ His
Son*. Only One life has ever won the victory over death; only
one kind of life ever can win it—that kind which was in
Him, which *is* in Him, which *He shares with all whom faith
makes one with Him*."

New Testament writers take "the life that now is, and
of that which is to come" and knot them together in one
bundle for the believer. Through grace he does not have
to wait until he dies, or is caught up to meet the Lord in
the air to enter upon Eternal Life. This blessed life commences at the New Birth, and every regenerate heart has
Heaven within to go to Heaven with.

> The men of grace have found
> Glory begun below.
> Celestial fruit on earthly ground
> From faith and hope may grow.

John makes it clear that this Eternal Life is not *something* but SOMEONE. "This life is *in* His Son" (1 John 5:
11, 12), or "This life *is* His Son" for "he that hath the Son
hath life, and he that hath not the Son hath not life". Did
not the Saviour say, "*I* am the Life"? Christ in us, then, is
the hope of Glory (Col. 1: 27). Do these glorious truths,
not only comfort our hearts, but wean them from this
changing world-order and fix them upon the heavenly and
eternal? Are we living in the light of Eternity? If so, then
we shall live as unto God here and now, and have a truer
perspective on crises whether personal or national, and a
worthier sense of values. "We shall not mistake imitation
gems for priceless jewels; nor shall we throw away eternal
gains for momentary thrills." May grace be ours to num-
ber our days and apply our hearts unto wisdom, and live
as children of the dawn, with our faces toward sunrise!
We may be living nearer Heaven than we think, and a
minute after death will answer all our questions on the

Life Beyond, and usher us into joys unspeakable and full of glory.

As the New Testament always approaches Heaven from a practical point of view, and never theoretically, presenting the truth as providing a moral force, it may be fitting to conclude our soul-absorbing meditation with a summary of the teaching of Christ and His Apostles. Turning to the attitude of Christ we distinguish these three aspects:

The Reality of Heaven becomes an Inspiration in the Formation of Character

He Who was rich but for our sakes became poor said: "Do not lay up treasures upon earth . . . Lay up treasures in Heaven". We cannot send our material wealth on ahead, nor take it with us. When a rich man dies the question is asked, How much did he leave? Why, he had to leave it all behind, and depart from the world as empty-handed as he entered it. Character is all we can take with us to the other side. Treasures we can deposit in Heaven's bank consist of holiness, faithfulness, utter devotion to Christ, and the reward accompanying the winning of the lost for Him.

The Reality of Heaven influences our Value of Others

It is profitable to trace how the Son of God from Heaven associated Heaven not only with possession but people.

> "See that you stumble not one of the least of these little ones, for their angels do always behold the face of My Father which is in Heaven."

Whether we think of "the little ones" as dear, innocent children or new-born souls in Christ makes no difference. Christ taught that we are to treat people here below more tenderly and humanely because of our relationship with the world beyond.

The Reality of Heaven is Identified with a Perfect Social Order on Earth

Coming from Heaven where He had lived from the dateless past and knew all about the perfect will of God, Jesus taught us to pray that God's will may be accomplished on earth, even as it is in Heaven. On earth as well as in Heaven, Jesus delighted to do His Father's will. There was never the slightest conflict between Father and Son. "My Father and I are one." In Heaven the angelic host and the myriads of saints of all ages obey implicitly the Divine will. What a different world ours would be if all rulers sought to know and obey the will of God for their peoples! Life can only be true, beautiful and harmonious as it is fashioned according to our Lord's Sermon on the Mount. When He returns to the earth as its rightful Lord and King then the prayer will be realized:

"Thy will be done on earth, as it is done in Heaven."

Turning to the Apostles we find that they are not less explicit in relating Heaven to earth, seeing that both form the Father's world.

In Heaven there is the Active Presence of Christ

Not only is He there preparing a place for a prepared people, He is at His Father's right hand as our Forerunner, our Representative, our Advocate, our Intercessor. He is up there to direct and inspire His people here below. He pleads our cause before the Father, as we plead His cause before a needy world. As the result of the promise of Christ, Heaven was not some distant sphere, but one quite close to them. Had He not said: "I will never leave thee, nor forsake thee"? Unseen, He is with us today, and will be until travelling days are o'er, undertaking for us by His heavenly grace and power.

In Heaven are Divine Principles Governing our Life on Earth

Paul reminds us that "our citizenship is in Heaven" or as *The Amplified Bible* expresses it, "We are citizens of the state-commonwealth, homeland—which is in Heaven". Already we have "joint seating with Him in the heavenly sphere" (Ephes. 2: 6). The term "politics" is derived from the word Paul uses for "citizenship". The real principles which should govern our life are not to be found in the world, with its differing shades of political thought, but in the purer politics of Heaven.

In Heaven we have God's Programme for Human Society

John predicts a new social order when God is all in all. "I saw a new heaven and a new earth: for the first heaven and the first earth were passed away" (Rev. 21: 1). Just how this perfect Universe of God will be constituted, and who the inhabitants of the new earth will be has not been revealed. There are those who dispose of Heaven with a sneer that "reflections upon Heaven are a waste of time". In the new order the Apostle envisages, falsehood will be unknown because of the enthronement of truth and righteousness. If only the nations of the present earth could be found ordering national life after the Divine Will, there would be more of Heaven on earth.

May we be permitted to conclude our dissertation on the Life Beyond on a more personal note? Have you recently had to say "Good-bye!" to a dear one who, while here below, walked in the fear of the Lord? You had no doubt whatever about the reality of their Christian faith as they conversed with you on things eternal. Theirs was a triumphant end, and you know that that loved one is with the Saviour above, and you hope for a blissful reunion in God's own time, but somehow you lack the assurance of salvation your now glorified friend experienced. Can it be that you have never known what it is to have a saving relationship with Christ? You are religious but not *Christian*. Yours has never been a definite committal to the claims of Christ. All He asks of you is the willingness to repent for your sin and open the avenues of your being for His entrance as your personal Saviour. If you die without Him as your Redeemer, how do you expect to meet your departed friend again?

> A dear one in Heaven, thy heart yearns to see,
>> At the beautiful gate may be watching for thee.
> Then list to this note of solemn refrain
>> "Ye must be born again".

Possibly the reader of these lines is a born-again believer with no doubt whatever about the possession of eternal life. Yet your heart is heavy with grief because one so precious to you is now in Heaven, and life is very lonely. You find it hard to adjust yourself to the vacant chair and often sigh for a touch of the familiar hand and the sound of the voice that is still. Rest assured that the Master who wept over the passing of Lazarus, whom He loved, understands your tears and waits to fill the vacant place in your heart with more of His own abiding presence. In the place of the one taken, He seeks to give you more of Himself.

> There is no place where earth's sorrows
> Are more felt than up in Heaven.

Let the God of all comfort sanctify your grief, and enable you to face the days with a calm and joyful resignation to the Divine will. Because His way is perfect, He never makes a mistake, never takes a wrong turning, never causes any child of His one unnecessary tear. So, cheer up! The days of separation will soon be over and when you come to cross the bar you, too, will see the Pilot face to face, and reunited with your dear one, praise Him for ever.

I shall see them again in the light of the morning.
When the night has passed by with its tears and its mourning;
When the light of God's love is the sun ever shining
    In the Land where the weary ones rest.

I shall know them again, though ten thousand surround them;
I shall hear their dear voice 'midst the blessed ones round them;
And the love that was theirs on the earth shall detect them,
    In the Land where the weary ones rest.

'Twas their lives in the past helped to fill me with gladness;
And the future in heaven, the home without sadness;
Where I see them today clad in bright robes of whiteness—
    In the Land where the weary ones rest.

Would I wish for them back from their bright home in heaven?
No! in patience I'll wait till the veil shall be riven,
And the Saviour restores me the friends He has given—
    In the Land where the weary ones rest.

E. Husband.

*   *   *

In Dr. Alexander Whyte's experience, the "terror of the Lord" and "the joy of His presence" were separated by so narrow a space. "What will it be to be there!" he exclaimed at the close of a rapturous passage on the bliss of the redeemed; and then, suddenly and solemnly he added, amid a silence which could be felt, "And what will it be NOT to be there!"